The
Flame
of the
Heart

Other
Breslov Research Institute Books
Published with Jewish Lights

*7th Heaven: Celebrating Shabbat
with Rebbe Nachman of Breslov*

*The Empty Chair: Finding Hope and
Joy — Timeless Wisdom from a Hasidic Master,
Rebbe Nachman of Breslov*

*The Gentle Weapon: Prayers for Everday
and Not-So-Everyday Moments — Timeless Wisdom
from the Teachings of the Hasidic Master,
Rebbe Nachman of Breslov*

*The Lost Princess and Other Kabbalistic
Tales of Rebbe Nachman of Breslov*

*The Seven Beggars and Other Kabbalistic
Tales of Rebbe Nachman of Breslov*

The
Flame
of the
Heart

Prayers of a
Chasidic Mystic

REB NOSON OF BRESLOV
TRANSLATED AND ADAPTED BY DAVID SEARS
with the BRESLOV RESEARCH INSTITUTE

For People of All Faiths, All Backgrounds
JEWISH LIGHTS Publishing
Woodstock, Vermont

The Flame of the Heart:
Prayers of a Chasidic Mystic

2006 First Jewish Lights Quality Paperback Edition
© 1999 by the Breslov Research Institute

Grateful acknowledgment is given for permission to use the material on pages 85, 88, 90, and 92 from the following source: *Compassion for Humanity in the Jewish Tradition* by David Sears, © 1998, used by permission of the publisher, Jason Aronson, Inc., Northvale, N.J., an imprint of Rowman & Littlefield Publishers, Inc., Lanham, MD.

Original paperback edition published by the Breslov Research Institute, Jerusalem/New York

Library of Congress Cataloging-in-Publication Data

Sternharz, Nathan, 1780–1844.
[Liòkuòte tefilot. English. Selections]
The flame of the heart : prayers of a Chasidic mystic / Reb Noson of Breslov ; translated and adapted by David Sears with the Breslov Research Institute.—1st Jewish Lights quality paperback ed.
p. cm.
Includes bibliographical references.
ISBN 1-58023-246-9
1. Judaism—Prayer-books and devotions—English. 2. Bratslav Hasidim—Prayer-books and devotions—English. I. Sears, David. II. Breslov Research Institute. III. Title.
BM665.S745213 2005
296.7'2—dc22
                                              2005030414

10 9 8 7 6 5 4 3 2 1

Manufactured in the United States of America

Published by Jewish Lights Publishing
A Division of Longhill Partners, Inc.
Sunset Farm Offices, Route 4, P.O. Box 237
Woodstock, VT 05091
Tel: (802)457-4000   Fax: (802)457-4004
www.jewishlights.com

Contents

Tikun: Self-Improvement

Deveykut: Cleaving to God

Hitbodedut: Meditation

Ma'aseh: Deeds

Shalom: Peace

Ge'ulah: Redemption

Acknowledgments

I would like to thank the people who helped to make this volume possible: Chaim Kramer for giving me the privilege of translating Reb Noson's prayers; Rabbi Symcha Bergman, who reviewed the essays and translations; Rabbi Ozer Bergman for his valuable suggestions; S. C. Mizrahi and Ruchama Feuerman, who edited the book; and Chava Shulman for assisting me with word-processing. Most of all, I thank my wife Shira, whose very name has the *gematria* (numerical value) of *tefilah* (prayer). And as the Kabbalists state, one's name reflects one's essence.

How to Use This Book

Look through the prayers in this book before you recite them, and choose any you feel in the mood to say. When it comes to the "service of the heart,"[1] sincerity is the main thing. If one of the prayers in this collection inspires you to add your own words to it, go right ahead. And if your words begin to flow, keep praying! (This practice, described below, is called *hitbodedut*. It was likewise Reb Noson's intention that his prayers be used as a springboard for *hitbodedut,* and that they not be treated as unalterable text.)[2]

The Baal Shem Tov (Rabbi Yisrael Ben Eliezer, founder of the Chasidic movement) taught: "Like a poor man, one should always address God with humble words of supplication."[3] This attitude is reflected in the plaintive tone of many of Reb Noson's prayers.

His words come from a heart that knows its own travail and so cries out to God. Other prayers in this collection flow from Reb Noson's joy in serving God or from his boundless love for God. Yet never does Reb Noson present God with insistent demands. "Be gracious unto me," he pleads. "But whatever You give me, I accept with love."

In the original version of these prayers, phrases such as "may I merit to be..." recur continually. This usage attests to the humility and simple piety of our Eastern European ancestors, who lived with the knowledge that everything is a gift from God. Nevertheless, the phrase "to merit" to attain this or that virtue or spiritual level does not fare well on the voyage from the author's culture to our own. For this reason, such usages have been omitted in this translation in a number of cases.

Another cultural barrier is encountered in Reb Noson's use of biblical quotations. The problem lies not in any difficulty the reader may have in relating to their content, which is as compelling today as ever. Rather, many readers may be unfamiliar with Judaism's sacred writings in their original Judaic frame of reference. They may sound foreign or archaic. Therefore, we have done our best to render these quotations in the modern idiom while remaining faithful to the classic biblical interpretations. Source references were omitted to avoid distracting the reader from the prayers.

Reb Noson, like Chasidim of his time, referred to God in the masculine. That approach is preserved in this edition of *The Flame of the Heart* to capture the prayers' authenticity. Also, these prayers were written by a Chasidic master and reflect the Jewish perspective and understanding of Torah ideals; they are, however, applicable universally. The prayers' messages extend to those of all faiths, all backgrounds.

This book was designed to guide and inspire the reader who wishes to pray. Beyond this, however, Reb Noson's prayers are highly instructive. Aside from their value to both practiced and occasional *daveners*, these prayers offer the reader a fairly good idea of what the Chasidic path is all about. May they help to draw us all near to God, wholeheartedly, in joy and in peace.

About These Prayers

REB NOSON

The author of these prayers is Rabbi Noson Sternhartz (1780–1844), foremost disciple of the celebrated Chasidic master Rebbe Nachman of Breslov (1772–1810). "Reb Noson," as he is known among Breslover Chasidim, lived in the Jewish Pale of Settlement during the Napoleonic era. Thus, while born into the traditional Jewish way of life and worldview, he experienced the revolution in societal values that, for most of us, has become part of everyday life.

The winds of secular humanism that swept through the world in the late 1700s threatened to supersede all organized religion, including Judaism. Despite the promise of greater social and economic freedom, the Jewish community was divided in its response to modern trends. On this issue, the young Reb Noson sided strongly with the religious traditionalists. But as to the dispute between the Chasidic and the non-Chasidic approaches to Jewish life and observance, he was unsure of where he stood.

Reb Noson came from a long line of Torah scholars. His father, Rabbi Naftali Hertz, was a respected textile merchant in the city of Nemirov, and his father-in-law, Rabbi Dovid Zvi Ohrbach, was chief rabbi of the cities of Sharograd, Kremenetz and Mohilev. Both were opponents of the Chasidic movement. As much as he respected his parents and teachers, Reb Noson could not unquestioningly accept their views on the hotly debated issue of Chasidism. Dissatisfied with his own spiritual life and seeking direction, he began to explore the Chasidic world. First he visited Rabbi Zusia of Anipoli, Rabbi Gedaliah of Linitz, Rabbi Barukh of Medzeboz, and others; then he spent a longer period of time in the court of Rabbi Levi Yitzchak of Berdichov. In his diary from that period, Reb Noson noted that he began to sense some progress in his spiritual quest, but still felt that something was missing.[1] Then a comrade spoke to him in glowing terms about a young Chasidic master who had recently moved to the region. Together, Reb Noson and his friend Reb Naftali traveled to meet

Rebbe Nachman in the nearby town of Breslov. There, Reb Noson found his teacher and his path.

After their first encounter in the fall of 1802, Rebbe Nachman remarked, "In every master-disciple relationship, the spiritual elements of Moses, Joshua and the Tent of Meeting are present."[2] These words of the Rebbe were prophetic: like Moses's disciple Joshua, Reb Noson "did not depart from the tent"[3] of his master for the rest of his life. Although already an accomplished scholar and a writer of great skill, Reb Noson came to Rebbe Nachman with the unbiased receptivity of a child who wants to learn the alphabet. Attesting to the high regard in which he held his gifted new disciple, the Rebbe stated: "I thank God for sending me a young man who will make sure that not another word of my teachings shall be lost."[4] It was Reb Noson who preserved and published Rebbe Nachman's works (as well as authoring many of his own, based on the teachings of his master). These core teachings have continued to inspire generations of Breslover Chasidim, as well as other spiritual seekers, to this day.[5]

Reb Noson exemplified what it means to be a Breslover Chasid. He truly lived with the Rebbe's teachings, plumbing their depths and applying their profound concepts as keys to open the gates to all other areas of Torah study and religious practice. Moreover, he realized that these teachings could serve as a lens through which to perceive the Divine life force and wisdom at each moment and in every situation. Reb Noson's approach to mysticism was not restricted to the intellectual realm; it was an all-encompassing path of knowledge. An eloquent testimony of this approach is his masterwork, *Likutey Halakhot*, a brilliantly woven tapestry of Talmudic law and Kabbalistic wisdom, interspersed with practical advice on making one's way through the mazes of both the outer and inner worlds.

Dedicated to the goal of improving the spiritual plight of others, Reb Noson accepted upon himself the difficult task of disseminating and explaining his master's wisdom. Thus, he was the paradigm of what in Breslov came to be known as the *manhig*—the living leader to whom other disciples turn for advice, instruction and guidance, now that the Rebbe is no longer a physical presence among us. (What is unique about this role in Breslov Chasidut is that, although the *manhig* may be a holy person in his own right, he is always looked upon as a more accomplished disciple, not a surrogate for Rebbe Nachman who had no successor. Through his writings and his disciples, Rebbe Nachman remains the leader of the Breslover Chasidim.)[6]

CHASIDIC PRAYER

The Chasidic masters wished to enable every Jew to experience *deveykut* — mystical communion with God. Therefore, they stressed prayer. *"Gohr mein zach iz tefilah* — My very essence is prayer," Rebbe Nachman declared. He spent most of his days in solitude, studying Torah, meditating and praying. Often Rebbe Nachman would go out to the fields and forests to commune with God. This practice, known as *hitbodedut* (from the root *badad*, meaning "solitary" or "alone"), was likewise stressed by his illustrious great-grandfather, the Baal Shem Tov, who founded the Chasidic movement some forty years before Rebbe Nachman was born.[7]

Following his master's example and instructions, Reb Noson devoted himself to prayer, both in the synagogue and alone, in the fields or at home. Eventually he committed to writing some of his original prayers, which were published under the title *Likutey Tefilot*. These excerpts from Reb Noson's prayers not only give us a glimpse into their author's inner life, but also serve to teach us how to pray.

The formalized prayer service has many advantages. While articulating the central concerns of Jewish life, it reinforces the social and spiritual bonds of the Jewish community. Yet the one precious component that was inevitably compromised when the prayer service became fixed is that of spontaneity. Rebbe Nachman sought to restore this by advocating the regular practice of *hitbodedut*. Spontaneity in prayer goes hand in hand with sincerity and fervor. The Rebbe looked upon spontaneous personal prayer as a powerful tool to aid one's spiritual work, especially when one prays in a secluded place late at night, when one can feel truly alone with God. If approached in the proper way, this practice can enable one to attain the highest levels of *deveykut*. Through a combination of self-examination and pouring out one's heart to God, it is possible to peel away the layers of the "false self," allowing the Infinite Light to illuminate one's consciousness.[8]

This is not to belittle the importance of the formal prayers. The Baal Shem Tov stated that he had reached his lofty spiritual levels primarily through prayer[9]—he viewed the daily prayer service as a path of mystical ascent. Thus, he taught his disciples to approach the daily prayer services with great fervor, attuning their minds and hearts to each word they recited, until they would reach a state of *deveykut*.[10] In keeping with the mystical teachings of the Ari (Rabbi Yitzchak Luria, the preeminent sixteenth century Kabbalist), he pointed out that the four sections of the prayer service parallel the "four worlds," or levels of reality, described in Kabbalistic literature.[11] If a person approaches the prayer service in a meditative manner, explained the Baal Shem Tov, then by the time he reaches the *Amidah* (Prayer of Silent Devotion), he will have achieved a higher state of consciousness. (Of course, the nature and quality of this experience will depend upon each individual's other spiritual attainments. Clearly, though, a prayer that is recited with mental focus and emotional sincerity is far more potent than one recited by rote.)

In practice, the Baal Shem Tov's approach to prayer is not as easy as it may seem. It takes great determination and stamina to imbue the written word with the breath of life. Also, it is often hard to find a *minyan* (quorum) conducive to this sort of *davening.* There are no easy solutions to these problems, but one thing is certain: when a person practices *hitbodedut* diligently, praying in the synagogue becomes a far more uplifting experience. There is a saying commonly displayed in synagogues: "Know before Whom you stand." The person who practices *hitbodedut* knows.

"MAKE MY TEACHINGS INTO PRAYERS"
As *manhig* (leader) of the Breslover Chasidim following the Rebbe's untimely death, Reb Noson endured

fierce opposition. One of the objections of his antagonists was that he had composed "a new prayer book."[12] In truth, the prayers he composed and published in *Likutey Tefilot* were never intended to usurp the established prayers. Nor, for that matter, was their recitation meant to take the place of *hitbodedut*. They were offered simply as a source of inspiration and direction for others to follow, especially helpful to those who would embark upon Rebbe Nachman's path.[13]

The inspiration for *Likutey Tefilot* was a directive of the Rebbe himself. "I would like you to compose prayers based on my teachings," he once told a group of his Chasidim.[14] Reb Noson began to do so almost immediately. Eventually this led to the authorship of *Likutey Tefilot*. Although portions of this work were confiscated by the Russian censors and subsequently lost, *Likutey Tefilot* contains prayers Reb Noson composed based on most of the discourses in Rebbe Nachman's magnum opus, *Likutey Moharan*. It is significant that, while Reb Noson published only one of the eight volumes of *Likutey Halakhot* during his lifetime, he published the entire text of *Likutey Tefilot*.[15]

A profound concept underlies the Rebbe's request to turn his teachings into prayers. A Chasidic discourse is not a dry, academic dissertation; it is a medium for the transmission of spiritual knowledge. Nevertheless, all knowledge is necessarily limited. Prior to its revelation, the concepts contained within a given discourse had been utterly bound up with the Infinite. This sublime level can be only "touched and not touched," as the Kabbalists state—known and yet not known. The inherent problem is that the mind that seeks knowledge becomes its own obstacle. The Infinite can be reached only by transcending the rational mind—by arriving at a state of "not knowing." One way of engaging in "not knowing" is through action: particularly through the performance of the *mitzvot* with joy.[16] Another way is through meditative prayer. Thus, when one "turns a teaching into a prayer," one employs the "revealed world" of the Chasidic discourse as a lens through which to perceive the "hidden world" of the Divine Oneness.[17]

Rebbe Nachman told his Chasidim: "I am taking you on a path that no man has ever traveled before. It is a very old path—yet it is completely new."[18] Rebbe Nachman's path is "new," because it vividly illuminates the present moment; yet it is "old," for it emanates from the highest, transcendent source of creation. Reb Noson's prayers also express this "old-new" quality, inasmuch as they represent the manner in which a

התעוררות

Hitorerut

Spiritual Awakening

SPIRITUAL UPS AND DOWNS

Help me, God, to be strong and determined in serving You; never let me fall. "Do not cast me away from Your Presence; do not take Your spirit of holiness away from me." Grant me the skill to engage in spiritual ascent—to attain the higher states of mystical perception—and grant me the skill to return to the mundane and to serve You through the simple tasks of everyday life. Help me to find You everywhere, for "if I rise up to Heaven, You are there, and if I make my bed in the abyss, behold, You are there." May I always cleave to You, and in my relationship with You, let me experience the fulfillment of the verse, "I am my Beloved's, and my Beloved is mine."

(1:56)

3

BEGINNING ANEW

Help us to serve You always, with all our hearts. May our Divine service seem new to us every day; may we begin afresh, as if we had never served You before. May we never succumb to thinking of ourselves as old or incapable of change; rather, may we be "bold as a leopard and light as an eagle, swift as a deer and strong as a lion, to carry out the will of our Father in Heaven." Let us experience the truth of the prophet's words, "Those who yearn for God will find their strength renewed; they will take flight like eagles; they will run and not become faint, walk and not become weary."

(I:776)

REMEMBERING THE FUTURE

"I remember my song in the night; with my heart I shall speak, and my spirit shall seek. I have remembered Your Name in the night, O God, and I shall heed Your teachings. I remember that God brings everything into existence when I recall Your wonders of old. I remember the days of old; I meditate upon Your deeds; about the work of Your Hands I shall speak. When my soul became faint, I remembered God. My soul remembers well and is humbled."

I encourage my soul: "Remember and do not forget that there is a World to Come and that this world has no permanence. This world passes in the blink of an eye—like a passing shadow, a swirl of dust, a vaporous cloud, a gust of wind, a fleeting dream. A person's life and true home is only the World to Come.

Have mercy on yourself, and guard your memory well; remember that world every day—never forget it. Let your thoughts cleave to the World to Come, and never let your awareness of that Supernal World leave you. Gaze deeply into yourself, and attain true presence of mind—for a person's stay in this world is but a fleeting moment."

I come before You, my God, to cast my supplications before Your mercy and to raise my eyes expectantly toward Your great kindness. Guard my memory well, and let me always remember the World to Come, binding my thoughts only to the World that endures forever.

Every day when I awaken from sleep, as soon as I open my eyes, may I remember my ultimate destiny. For this world is empty and without substance, "a fleeting vapor—vanity of vanities, all is vanity." There is no gain from all the labors that one exerts in worldly endeavors, for there is no purpose or true good to be found in this world except the diligent pursuit of the World to Come. Grant me the presence of mind to remember this well through the power of holy remembrance.

In every time and place, enable me to understand the hidden messages that You constantly send in order to draw me close to You in truth. For in Your great kindness, You have constricted Your Godliness from the first point of Creation, the beginning point of the World of Emanation (*Atzilut*) to the center point of this physical World of Action (*Asiyah*)—from the Infinite to the finite. Through this constriction, You send hidden messages to each person, in every situation, to bring him or her closer to Your service, in accordance with the place, the time and the individual. Open my mind that I may clearly understand these hidden messages. Thus I will return to You in truth; now and forever I will fulfill Your will.

Teach me and guide me, in Your great kindness and awesome power, that I may attain the higher levels of consciousness necessary to understand these hidden messages. At the same time, grant me the wisdom to constrain this higher consciousness, that it never exceed its proper bounds.

Let me not inquire into the mysteries that are above my ability to understand or search out what must remain hidden to me. Help me to contemplate only that which lies within my limits; may I increase my wisdom in a modest, measured way, according to my spiritual level. In this way I will recognize and understand, at all times and at every moment, all the

REKINDLING THE FLAME

Master of the Universe, Knower of Secrets: You know all the mysteries of the world; You know the secrets of all living creatures. What can I say before You? Nothing is concealed from You, nothing hidden from Your sight.

Eternal One, Awesome One, Lofty One, before Your Presence the universe with all it contains is as nothing, and all of time does not amount even to the blink of an eye. You alone understand the nature of Your mercy: how You wish to confer upon us the ultimate goodness, which is to know Your truth, to experience an illumination of Eternity, an illumination of Your Godliness and Your awesome wonders, the sublime delight of cleaving to Your Oneness.

How many incarnations have You granted us, how

many diverse happenings and chains of cause and effect—sometimes pleasant, sometimes painful—have You brought about, all for our ultimate benefit? For everything in life is meant to awaken us to serve You in truth, to encourage us to renounce our evil deeds and character traits, to draw near to You and to cleave to You, to become sated with Your goodness and illuminated with transcendent lights. May we "gaze upon the pleasantness of God and meditate in His palace," and perceive Your Oneness. This is the ultimate success, the ultimate deliverance, the ultimate benefit and the ultimate goal.

Who would believe that someone such as myself—created to receive such goodness, to attain such a sublime goal, to delight in God and take refuge in the shadow of His Presence—could commit such deeds as my deeds and conceive such thoughts as my thoughts? What can I say? In truth, I have no words with which to justify myself. All I can do is cry out with a bitter voice over my spiritual devastation, until God looks down upon me in His mercy. For nothing can deter God's salvation, which can come at any moment. His deliverance is absolute and true, a deliverance that lasts forever.

Therefore, may it be Your will, our God and God of our ancestors, that the merit and power of the true *tzaddikim* shine upon us. Through their merit may we experience true joy. Through their great inspiration may the spirit of enlightenment come upon us. Awaken us from our spiritual sleep, and remove from our hearts all sadness and depression, insensitivity and lethargy. Then our souls will burn with fervor, enflamed with true longing for You.

(II:212–13)

TURNING DARKNESS
INTO LIGHT

O God, Whose goodness never ceases, may I be worthy of receiving Your true goodness. Satisfy the deepest desire of my soul and enable me to merge into Your Oneness—to reach the ultimate state of self-nullification and spiritual harmony. May I progress along the spiritual path, like the angels in Ezekiel's vision, "advancing and then returning"—advancing toward the eternal and retreating toward the temporal world—until I attain the full realization that everything in life is a manifestation of pure goodness and that evil does not really exist. For when one contemplates that all suffering and affliction is in fact hidden goodness, the disguise of suffering falls away. Help me accept whatever suffering I must endure with love and joy, and enable me to nullify its painful aspect through binding myself to the Ultimate Reality, which is true goodness.

(I:805)

FINDING GOD WHEREVER ONE STANDS

God of Heaven, God of Earth, All-Powerful One, Who encompasses everything: Shine the holy light of the true *tzaddikim* upon us, the light that shines through all the worlds, both spiritual and physical. Enlighten both those who dwell above and those who dwell below. Reveal to those who dwell above, who have attained a higher level of holiness, that they have not begun to know God at all. Arouse and awaken all those who dwell below in the dust, on the lowest spiritual level, with the perception that "the entire earth is full of God's glory." Raise up these fallen souls from wherever they have fallen. Restore their spirits and awaken them, even those who have fallen to the farthest depths through their evil deeds and transgressions. Let Your compassion reach them all.

Encourage the weak and the spiritually injured, the sinful and the embittered, and bring them back to You. Have pity on the poor and destitute — save them, awaken them and give them strength, that they not despair, for God may be found everywhere. Even from the depths of the abyss it is possible to come closer to You, "for there is no place devoid of You" and no cause in the world for despair.

Awaken me, O God, awaken me; be gracious to me and raise me up. "Set my feet upon the rock; firmly support my steps." Grant me the strength to revere You and serve You. "Neither cast me off nor abandon me, God of my deliverance." Fortify me in my weakness, that I may return to You in truth. May I trust in You, God, and never falter, nor become disheartened for any reason. "Behold, God is my deliverance; I shall trust and not fear, for God is my strength and my song, and He has been my salvation."

May I be worthy to fully realize that "the whole world is full of God's Glory." Then I shall live with a constant sense of Your Presence and truly know and believe that Your Glory fills the world. For You both permeate all worlds and transcend all worlds, and there is no place from which You are absent. "'If a person conceals himself in hidden places, do I not see him?' declares God. 'Indeed, do I not fill the heavens and the earth?'" Help me to fulfill the words of the verse "I place God before me constantly" by knowing, discerning and sensing Your awe and the truth of Your existence; for You stand before us continually, and nothing is hidden from Your sight.

Enable us all to realize the unity of both perceptions of God: the exalted perception of those who dwell below—that no place is empty of His Presence; and that of those who dwell above—the Heavenly hosts who exclaim, "Where is the place of His Glory?" For no thought can grasp You at all, and that ultimate knowledge of God lies in "not knowing," for His greatness cannot be fathomed.

(II:164, 166)

THE LONG JOURNEY

Merciful One, raise me up from a beast-like existence to a human existence — from body to soul, from matter to spirit, from darkness to light, from foolishness to intelligence, from false intellect to the holy wisdom of Torah, from forgetfulness to memory. Call forth that faculty of "memory" which stems from Your Essence and instill it within me.

Let me always remember all the words of Your Torah and Divine service: those I have learned from sacred texts and those I have heard or will hear from my teachers and friends. Help me remember clearly everything that relates to the fear of God, to Torah and Divine service; let me never forget anything I have learned.

May I always remember my mortal destiny and

take to heart the purpose for which my soul descended to this lowly world. May I constantly bear in mind what will happen to me when my days come to an end. Help me to remember this well every day; for all our days and years are without substance—like a fleeting dream, a passing shadow, a vaporous cloud, a gust of wind and a swirl of dust.

It is impossible to elude death, no matter where one turns: "There is no escape from this war." What can one possibly say before God? What can one do when the day of destiny arrives? "My soul remembers well and is humbled"—for there is no forgetfulness before the Divine Throne, and nothing is hidden from God's sight. Help me remember this always, so that I will tend to my soul's deepest needs and save myself from destruction. May I prepare "sustenance" for the journey of my soul, for "the way is long, and even scant provisions are lacking."

(1:543)

MUSIC TO AWAKEN
THE SOUL

Deliver me from illusory goodness, which in the end is bitter as gall and wormwood. Grant me Your enduring goodness, O God, that I may be happy in all circumstances. "I shall rejoice in Your deliverance, and Your melodies I shall play on musical instruments in God's Temple, all the days of my life." Let me raise my voice in exalted song and melody for the sake of Your Name, according to Your beneficent will.

May I always awaken and reveal the Ten Kinds of Song, with which the Book of Psalms is written. Let me hear the melody and song of true joy in Divine service from a skillful and spiritually refined musician—"a singer with a beautiful voice, who plays the instrument well." For such a musician knows how to play holy melodies which are drawn forth from the harp of King David.

Such a musician can separate the "good spirit"—a spirit of prophecy, a spirit of enlightenment, a spirit of joy and gladness—from the "evil spirit," a spirit of sadness, a spirit of grief. Then we will all attain true happiness and will return to You with a whole heart, for the heart is opened through holy joy and melody.

(1:669)

THE TRUE GOAL

May I always seek to come close to You, O God, and not be deceived by the vain attractions of this world. What can be gained by the pursuit of wealth? Will it not all be taken from me when I die? "For nothing accompanies a person when he passes away, not silver, gold, precious gems or pearls; only Torah and good deeds." Whether or not I succeed in acquiring riches, I will have wasted my days for naught. "What does a person gain from all his efforts that he labors under the sun? Utter emptiness; all is emptiness."

Even if I am unworthy to serve You due to my many sins, may my desire to draw near to You still remain strong and my holy determination never diminish. May You perform wonders for me and draw me near to You in truth.

(II:83)

תיקון

Tikun

Self-Improvement

SIMPLICITY

O God, teach me the ways of wholeheartedness and simplicity. May I be "wholehearted with my God" and perform His will with devotion, with a faith that is simple and straightforward, without cleverness or sophistication. For You know that there is no way to approach You except through absolute simplicity, through sincerity and complete faith.

Even in the depths of our spiritual decline, in the bitterness of our exile, there are paths of simplicity through which we may derive new life. Through simplicity we can find a straight path and spiritual direction—for it is possible to find God in every place and in all situations, no matter how far we may have fallen.

Every person can appease You through simplicity in prayer and supplication, through sincerity and simple faith; for this is Your desire, as we have been told: "My eyes are upon the faithful of the land, that they may dwell with Me; those who walk the simple path are the ones who shall serve Me."

(II:440)

PRAYING FOR THE WORLD

May we always pray for the entire world's welfare and the fulfillment of its needs. Through our prayers, may all harsh decrees against the world be annulled. In Your great mercy, grant us the knowledge of whether it is before or after the sealing of Heaven's decree, that we may know how to entreat You. Show us how to garb our prayers in ordinary conversation at those times when it is not acceptable to approach You directly through prayer. Yet if at such times we remain far from this knowledge and perception, we know that our destiny always remains in Your hands, and nothing can interfere with Your will. "O God, never withhold Your mercy from me; may Your kindness and truth always protect me."

(I:48)

OVERCOMING ANGER

O God, Who is full of goodness, mercy and favor, deliver me from anger and irritability. Even if I become angry, God forbid, have pity on me in Your great mercy, and prevent me from doing anything cruel. May I overcome my burning emotions and break my anger with mercy. Help me show mercy when I wish to vent my rage. May I harbor no "strange god" within myself, for an angry person is compared to an idol worshiper.

Master of the Universe: You know how hard it is to break this evil trait of anger. As soon as anger begins to burn within us, we nearly lose control altogether; it is so difficult to extinguish the fire of anger. Have mercy on us for the sake of Your Name. Help us remove anger and irritability from our hearts and never again succumb to these feelings. May we emulate the Divine attribute of seeking the good of all living creatures, now and forever.

(I:261–262)

TRUTH

God of Truth, imbue me with the truth that flows from Your Essence. From this moment on, turn me from falsehood to truth; thus may I grasp the Absolute Truth. Draw forth Your Divine providence upon me; watch over me with a loving and gracious eye until I return to You in truth. Then the reality of "After Creation"—temporal existence—will become one with the reality of "Before Creation," the source of all existence in eternity; and everything will be revealed as perfect Oneness, perfect truth.

(1:643)

THE BEST MEDICINE

Master of the Universe, Source of all joy: "Gladden the soul of Your servant; for unto You, my Master, I lift up my soul." Help me know the ways of true joy, that I may enlist all depression and grief to join the dance of my gladness. Thus may all forms of sadness, all sighs and groans, be transformed into joy. Enable me always to strengthen and encourage myself with great joy, to arouse the Ten Kinds of Song through which holy joy finds full expression. Let me gladden my soul constantly with happy melodies. Then I will rejoice and sing to God with songs and praises, chants and hymns and melodies, and I will be always full of joy.

Through joy, may I draw into myself the life force of holiness, strengthening thereby all Ten Pulses which are found within me. Thus may I be protected from all sickness, disease and injury, both physical and spiritual, for all of these come from sadness and depression. Heal me and all of Your people, Israel; grant us health and life through joy and gladness. This can heal all the diseases in the world, for joy is a person's life force. "Heal us and we shall be healed, save us and we shall be saved, for You are our praise. Bring healing to all our illnesses, all our sufferings and all our ailments," healing of the body and healing of the soul.

(II:284)

THE ESSENCE OF
THE SOUL

May I strengthen myself with great joy at all times, achieved through every sort of strategy and advice by which to gladden the heart. Whether by striving to find the good points in myself and in others, or even by humorous behavior, such as harmless jokes, clowning and the like, may I bring myself to joy, for this is our main source of holiness and vitality.

Merciful One, Creator of Healing, Master of Wonders, Who redeems us through joy, instill joy in our hearts, for You know all the secrets of our hearts. You know the many strategies the Evil Inclination constantly devises to defeat us by casting us into depression. The Evil Inclination is amazingly adept at tricking us, even dressing itself in the guise of *mitzvot* in order to make us think we are unhappy for good reason, such as making us feel depressed over our transgressions.

In truth, this is all a trap, for we have already been taught that it is enough to set aside one hour a day for self-examination—to pour out our hearts to God concerning whatever we have been through. However, the rest of the day we are to strengthen ourselves with joy. At times we must force ourselves to be happy; for the essence of the soul is joy.

Have mercy on us. May we understand and know intuitively the various paths and strategies by which to remain joyous at all times. Enable us to live by Your decrees and to heed Your *mitzvot* "with joy and with a whole heart, recognizing the abundance of good," until we attain the true joy of the Ultimate Future.

May we be worthy of gazing upon the joyous circle that the *tzaddikim* will form, when each will point with his finger and say, "This is God!" As it is written: "On that day they will declare, 'Behold, this is our Lord for Whom we have waited. He has saved us! This is God for Whom we have waited. Let us celebrate and rejoice in His deliverance.'"

Then the words of the prophet Isaiah will be speedily fulfilled: "God's redeemed ones shall return and come to Zion in glad song, crowned with eternal joy. Happiness and joy they shall possess, and sorrow and sighing will disappear. For with joy you shall go out, and in peace you shall be led forth; the mountains and hills will burst forth in song before you, and all the trees of the field will clap hands. For God has consoled Zion, consoled all her ruins. He has made her wilderness like Eden and her desert like God's garden. Joy and gladness will flourish there, thanksgiving and song."

(II:285–287)

THE SPIRIT OF THE
TZADDIKIM

Merciful God, may the merit of the true *tzaddikim* protect me. Through them, enable me to eradicate any sense of self-importance, until the realization of my truly humble station pervades every limb of my body. Help me attain true humility and complete faith, so that not even a trace of pride will enter my mind or heart. Help me to overcome all spiritual confusion and doubts; may such feelings never arise in my heart or in anyone's heart.

Let the enlightened spirit of the true *tzaddikim* reach me. May I draw deeply from the wellsprings of their wisdom. Thus the crookedness of my heart will be made straight, and my heart will always be attuned to Godliness, in truth, in complete faith and in humility.

Cause this spirit of enlightenment to reach my

hands and my feet, purifying them from all spiritual imperfection. Reveal the light of the *tzaddikim* and let it shine forth. May my heart light up with joy for the sake of Your Name, until the joy spreads to my hands and feet, and I clap and dance in holy ecstasy. Thus, all harsh judgments will be overturned, and love and compassion will prevail.

(1:117–118)

REGAINING ONE'S TRUE FACE

Master of the Universe, Who knows all the thoughts of my heart, what shall I say before You, Who sits in the loftiest heights? What shall I relate before You, Who dwells in the highest heavens? You know the mysteries of the universe and the secrets of all living creatures. You search through our inner recesses and examine every corner of our hearts. Nothing is hidden from You; nothing is concealed from Your sight. Beneficent One Who is good to all, fill us with Your goodness, and instill in us the trait of being good to all.

Forgive me for all my mistakes, transgressions and sins; forgive me for all the physical and spiritual harm I have caused through my anger. Have mercy on me and deal with me according to Your true goodness. Be with me always and deliver me, that I never become angry or irritable, even in my heart, toward anyone or anything in the world. Enlighten me with the light of Your Face, and in Your mercy restore that higher dimension of consciousness which I lost on account of my sins. Confer upon me the Divine image — the shining face of the Living King. In Your kindness and grace, enlighten me with holy wisdom (*Chokhmah*), with understanding (*Binah*) and with knowledge (*Daat*), so that I will be able to radiate spirituality and shine forth to others.

May I become a human being in the truest sense. Help me overcome my animalistic tendencies and fully attain the level of a human. Then fear will grip the predatory beasts of the earth and all those who seek to harm me, as it is written, "Your fear and terror shall be upon all the beasts of the earth. Let Your face shine upon Your servant; deliver me in Your kindness. Let Your face enlighten Your servant; teach me Your statutes."

(I:715)

THE PATH OF RETURN

Master of the Universe, Cause of all causes, Who brings about all things: You transcend everything, and nothing transcends You. No thought can grasp You. "Unto You silence is praise," for You are above all blessings and praises.

For this I beseech You, for this I entreat You: pave a clear path, a path that traverses all the worlds and spiritual levels, even to the place where I stand, according to the true good that is revealed to You alone, Knower of Secrets. Through this path, cause Your Light to shine upon me, and bring me back to You with a whole heart, as if I had requested this with the pure desire of one who is spiritually refined. Do not let my mind be disturbed by impure thoughts, or by any confusion or any thought that is contrary to Your will.

Let my thoughts cleave only to worthy and holy matters, to Divine service, Divine perception and Divine wisdom.

Incline my heart to Your Torah, and instill a pure heart within me, that I may serve You in truth. From the depths of the sea rescue me without a moment's delay—for "God's deliverance comes in the blink of an eye." May I be illuminated by the Light of Life all my days on the face of the earth.

May I renew the days of my youth, the days when I wandered in darkness, and restore them to the realm of holiness; thus may my departure from the world be like my birth, without sin. God, bestow Your favor upon me, that I may gaze upon Your pleasantness and explore Your palace, where everything declares Your glory.

(Reb Noson's manuscript)

דביקות

Deveykut
Cleaving to God

THE SPIRIT OF ENLIGHTENMENT

Master of the Universe: have mercy upon us and hear our prayers. Anoint us with Divine Intellect—the holy intuition of transcendent reality, the spirit of enlightenment. Reveal to us the light of Divine intellect in a flash of higher perception. May we merit to grasp the supernal wisdom which is known as the "Light of the Divine Face," so that all explanations and techniques will no longer be necessary.

May the constant influx of Divine Intellect cause the flame of the heart to rise of its own accord. Thus may our hearts be always enflamed with awe of God and fervor in Divine service, with flames of Divine fire. Through the heart's holy fervor, may we rectify all the spiritual damage we have caused in the past through the fire of our negative character traits and of our burning physical desires.

"Create in me a pure heart, O God, and renew in me a proper spirit. Do not cast me away from before You, and do not take Your holy spirit from me."

(1:342)

GRASPING THE INFINITE

In Your great love and compassion, You have allowed the true *tzaddikim* to bring the light of Godliness into our minds and our intellects—constricting Yourself into the letters of the Torah, which is the root of prophecy. This is the mystical meaning of the verse "You ascended Above and took a captive," which refers to the Torah that Moses took as a "captive" from Heaven and gave to the Children of Israel. Have mercy on us for the sake of Your Name, and enable the *tzaddikim* to complete the healing of our souls and to reveal Godliness to us. Help us cleave to You in thought, through study of Your holy Torah, night and day. Thus may our mortal minds grasp Godliness, in holiness and in purity, in awe and in trembling, and may we fulfill the prophet's words, "I held Him and would not let Him go."

(II:529)

FINDING GOD IN EVERYTHING

Have mercy upon me, Merciful God, and lead me through the confusion of this world, along the path of truth. May all my actions and endeavors, even my smallest movements—as well as those of my children, my descendants and all who depend upon me—reflect Your will alone. In Your great mercy, help me strengthen the kingdom of holiness, and let the inclination for good within me overcome my evil inclination. Be gracious to me, and pour forth Your wisdom upon me. Then I will be able to perceive everything with the light of Higher Consciousness, and cleave to God through everything the world contains—to decipher the countless hidden messages You have woven into the fabric of everyday life, to bring me closer to You.

(I:5)

THE HEART OF THE WORLD

Deliver us and protect us, in Your great mercy, from the storm wind of the soul, that the intensity of our fervor never overwhelm us. This is called "breaking through," as the verse warns: "Let them not break through to ascend to God." In the power and merit of the true *tzaddikim*, draw upon us the holiness of the prophet Elijah, who rode on fiery horses in a storm wind; for his power can also enable us to contain the fire which burns through the storm of excessive fervor.

In truth, we don't know how far to let our feelings take us; we have no idea how to maintain the delicate balance of fervor and restraint. Sometimes our hearts are completely closed and unfeeling; at other times we become carried away with emotion. There is no one upon whom we can rely other than our Father in

Heaven and the true *tzaddikim;* for the *tzaddik* is called "one who has spirit—who knows how to respond to the spirit of every person."

May the enlightened spirit of the true *tzaddikim* illuminate each one of us. Through this spirit of holiness and purity may we experience true joy, as is Your will. Then every heart will be filled with longing for You, according to each person's nature and spiritual level.

The entire House of Israel who are the "heart of the world" will truly function as a heart, wherever the pulse of holiness needs to be felt. Then all of humanity will cleave to You and will be enflamed with holy fervor, until all Creation reveals Your Oneness. Thus the words of the Torah will be fulfilled, "And you who cleave to the Lord your God—you are all alive today."

(II:214–215)

CLEAVING TO GOD

God of Truth, may I come to believe in You in truth. Through faith may I come to experience Godliness and cleave to You forever. Help me recognize my own smallness and always remain aware of Your Presence, for without God it is impossible to lift a hand or a foot. In all my deeds, even while eating and drinking, help me cleave to You, so that all my actions shall be for Your sake.

May I always remember You—when I lie down and when I arise, when I am at home and when I go on the way, in silence and in speech. Whether I am involved in spiritual pursuits or in worldly affairs, may I hold fast to You and never forget You.

(1:64)

ONENESS RETURNS TO ONENESS

Enable us to fulfill the precept of "unto Him you shall cleave." Have mercy on us and grant us the ultimate spiritual level: that of true self-nullification. Then we will become one with God, which is the purpose of all Creation. "God of Hosts, return to us; cause Your Face to shine, and we will be redeemed. Return to us, O God, and we will return to You; renew our days as before," when all was Oneness.

(1:649)

התבודדות

Hitbodedut

Meditation

PRAYING IN THE FIELDS

"Come, Beloved, let us go out to the field; let us lodge in the villages. Let us arise early to go to the vineyards; let us see if the vine has blossomed, if the tender grapes have opened, if the pomegranates have sprouted. There I will give my love to You."

Master of the Universe, let me seclude myself in meditation and prayer every day, going out to the fields to meditate among the trees and grass, pouring out my heart in prayer. For all the leaves and grass, all the trees and plants, will stir themselves to greet me; they will rise to imbue my words and prayers with their energy and life force. All the trees and plants of the field will merge with my words and prayers; they will combine all their spiritual power and bring my words up to their supernal

Source. Thus my prayers and supplications will attain perfection.

O Merciful One, may I merit to pray before You, until my heart opens at last. May my words flow until I pour out my heart like water before God.

(II:224)

MIDNIGHT MEDITATION

"My soul longs for You in the night; the spirit within me seeks You. I have remembered Your Name at night, O God, and I have kept Your Torah. I remember my song in the night; with my heart I commune, and my spirit seeks."

Master of the Universe Who is One, Singular and Unique, transcending past, present and future: You created this world and all the supernal Universes, according to Your beneficent will. You sent forth our souls to this world to serve You in truth, thus to reveal Your kingship. Through our positive actions we can spiritually elevate all worlds, from the lowest level of the World of Action to the highest level of the World of Emanation. We can elevate everything to its supernal Source, so that every element of the universe will merge into Your absolute Oneness.

Therefore show me mercy and enable me to spend much time in secluded meditation every day, until I attain self-nullification—the complete eradication of the ego. Then I will be able to merge with Your Oneness in truth.

Allow me a special place and a special time for my meditations—a secluded path late at night, while most people are sleeping. May I go there every night, to that secluded path where people do not go, even by day. There, let me meditate and put my thoughts and feelings into words, pouring out my heart to You, until my heart yearns for You and my eyes flow with tears. May I confess all of my many failings before You, regretting them all truly and sincerely, and resolve not to return to my foolish ways again.

Help me—not because I have earned Your favor, but because of Your great mercy. Protect me from all misdeeds, transgressions and selfish desires. Through my secluded meditations let me attain true self-nullification, so that I eradicate every negative character trait and every self-seeking desire, until I have completely cleansed myself of them all. Help me remove every trace of ego, until I reach the ultimate level of self-nullification and become incorporated within the Divine Oneness in truth.

Then all temporal existence will be integrated into the Essential Reality: everything will become one with God and exist within God forever, never to be separated from Him again. Your Oneness will be revealed throughout Creation. "And everything created will know that You created it, and everything formed will realize that You formed it. And everyone who breathes the breath of life shall declare: 'The Lord God of Israel is King, and His dominion is over all.'"

(I:647–648)

THE FLAME OF THE HEART

Rock of my heart, Creator of everything, Master of all that transpires, Lord of all souls Who knows all secrets: You know the holy Divine light that blazes in the depths of my heart—for our souls are a portion of God Above and Your Godliness dwells within us. Therefore my heart cries within me; it cries like a harp. "My heart longs, and even expires, for the court-yards of God; my heart and my flesh will sing unto the Living God."

The flame within me burns for You; deep waters cannot extinguish it, rivers cannot drown it. The light of my heart is one with Your Infinite light; it is limit-less—there is no end to my yearning for You. This longing is without measure and beyond compare.

The fire within me reaches to infinity; were I to

surrender to it, I would not be able to make a move, so great is my desire to become one with God. Yet You have revealed through Your holy Sages that this is not Your desire; this was not Your intent in creating us. For You know that we are but flesh and blood, and it is impossible for us to cleave to You constantly.

You desire all the various forms of our Divine service and good deeds, the study of Torah and the performance of its precepts, for which our souls were sent down to this physical world. Therefore You have commanded us "not to break through to ascend to God," but rather to constrain the light that blazes in our hearts, and to create within ourselves an "empty space," as it is written: "My heart is hollow within me." In this way, we will be able to instill within our hearts all good traits.

May we follow in Your ways and attach ourselves to Your holy attributes, serving You humbly, approaching You gradually, step by step. In this way we will wholeheartedly come to accept upon ourselves the yoke of Your kingdom and reveal Your Godliness to all of humanity, for the destiny of Creation is for all the world to come to know You.

(I:623)

LIVING WITH MINDFULNESS

Merciful God, grant me the ability to tame my mind. Imbue me with the holiness, purity and spiritual inspiration that flow from the level of the "Supernal Crown"— the Divine will—through which everything in the universe comes into being from nothingness. From this level, let me receive the power of holy restraint and mental focus. May I always live with mindfulness, in truth and in perfect faith, in holiness and purity, as is Your will.

Deliver me from base desires and fantasies, foreign thoughts and false wisdom. Help me attune the inner faculties of the mind—wisdom, understanding and knowledge—so that my mind never drifts toward any errant thought. May my mind always remain clear and pure.

Help me ascend from one spiritual level to the

next, through performing Your *mitzvot* with joy, until I reach the level wherein my thoughts flow only to You, in holiness and in purity, with true mindfulness and perfect faith. Source of all miracles and wonders, let my thoughts seek always to perceive the Infinite Light, which transcends the levels of my *nefesh*, *ruach*, and *neshamah*. May my soul be sated with transcendent lights. "One thing I ask of God, it is all that I seek: to dwell in the House of God all the days of my life, to gaze upon His pleasantness and to meditate in His sanctuary."

(I:393)

THE SUPERNAL CROWN

Protect me with the holy force that restrains and focuses the mind, that emanates from the level of the Supernal Crown; thus may I never venture beyond the bounds of holiness. Rather, let my thoughts flow toward the perception of the Infinite Light, in a manner of "advancing and returning," "reaching yet not reaching," "running while being held back" by the holy force that restrains and focuses the mind.

May I merit to elevate my consciousness, until it is subsumed within the Nine Supernal Palaces, of which it is taught: "They are neither lights nor spirits nor souls; no one can attain them or cleave to them or know them." For only You, God, know the yearnings of my *nefesh*, *ruach*, and *neshamah* in their Supernal Source—how they strive to experience these sublime levels of mystical perception, the attainment of which is the purpose of my existence. "My soul thirsts for the Lord, for the Living God; when will I come to see God's face? My soul yearns—and even expires—for the courtyards of God; my heart and my flesh will sing unto the Living God."

However, through my transgressions I have diverted these illuminations; my sins have caused Your face to be hidden from me; for my thoughts have followed evil passions and fantasies, as well as philosophical views contrary to Torah. I have damaged all the chambers of my intellect, all the pathways and channels that lead to higher perception; I have destroyed the house of wisdom, broken down the walls of understanding, demolished the palaces of knowledge. Through my countless misdeeds and transgressions I have greatly abused the faculties of my mind and the power of mental focus and restraint, the source of which is the Supernal Crown.

Therefore I cast my supplication before You, God of Forgiveness and Mercy. Forgive me as if I had adequately atoned for my many sins and transgressions. Lift me out of the depths of the sea, according to Your miraculous ways. Restore and perfect my mind. Deliver me at last from all foreign thoughts, from all evil fantasies, from all preoccupation with physical desires and worldly attachments.

Purify and sanctify me with Your sublime holiness; take away my sighs and groans, and eradicate completely every trace of depression. May I attain true joy, and perform Your *mitzvot* with the greatest enthusiasm and delight. Restore my spiritual ruins; rebuild the palaces of my intellect on their proper foundations. May the citadels of my mind be established in their rightful place, in holiness and purity, in truth and in perfect faith.

May I merit to progress quickly along the spiritual path, ascending from level to level until I reach the Nine Supernal Palaces. Then, even while in this world, I will recognize and know You in truth. May I merit to climb all the rungs of holiness, to reach the highest level that can be attained in this world. For this is the purpose of the soul's descent from the celestial heights to this lowly world: to merit, in accordance with the good deeds it performed while in the body, to return to that place from which it was taken—and even higher, with even more power, even more strength.

(I:393–395)

מעשה

Ma'aseh

Deeds

SERVING GOD WITH JOY

Instill in my heart true joy in serving You, as it is written: "Serve God with gladness, and rejoice in the midst of trembling." Enable me to perform all of Your *mitzvot* with the joy that comes from the essence of the mitzvah itself. May I delight and rejoice while performing each mitzvah, simply because of the honor of fulfilling Your will. May all my joy come only from the mitzvah itself, without any concern for ultimate reward.

Protect me from all base motives when I serve You. May thoughts concerning worldly gain or what other people might think of me never enter my mind. Rather, may I perform every mitzvah with the great joy of the mitzvah itself. May my gratification come only from serving You, such that I never desire any other recompense, even in the World to Come. For the greatest reward is the opportunity to perform yet another mitzvah, as our Sages have said: "The reward for a mitzvah is another mitzvah."

(I:46)

CONDUITS OF ONENESS

May we become one with You through the performance of Your holy *mitzvot,* which are conduits for
Your Oneness. Thus it is written, "God will rejoice in
His works... Israel will rejoice in its Maker." You will
rejoice in us because we have done that which is good
in Your sight, and we will delight and rejoice in You.

Through our joyous performance of the mitzvot,
may we draw life and blessing into the 248 limbs and
the 365 sinews of the body; may we likewise draw life
and blessing into the entire world and into the entire
cycle of the year, to encompass the three dimensions of
World, Year and Soul. Then all Creation will bless
You, and receive in return Your blessings of life, goodness, holiness and purity.

(1:47)

THE GOOD LIFE

O God, Who is sufficient unto Himself, help me to be content with whatever I have. May I involve myself in material pursuits as little as possible and be satisfied with the few possessions I need. And should You bless me with higher consciousness, that I perceive the spiritual dimension in every physical object, nevertheless, may I have not the least inclination to increase my worldly possessions. Let me rather content myself with only the most basic necessities, in holiness and purity. May my main striving be only in Divine service, purely for Your sake, so that I devote all my days to Torah study, prayer and good deeds.

Even if I earn just enough money to meet my basic expenses, grant me the ability to contribute to charity, so that I may fulfill the verse "Good is the man who is gracious and lends, who conducts his affairs with justice." Grant me the merit to give charity generously to worthy people in need. Through acts of charity we bring about the mystical unification of the Holy One, blessed be He, with the *Shekhinah* (Divine Presence) — the Divine aspect of giving with the Divine aspect of receiving — in perfect harmony.

(1:657)

THE WORLD IS GOD'S NAME

Master of the Universe, unify my divided heart to love and revere Your Name. Help me to mend my deeds and sanctify my thoughts so that I will be able to accomplish lofty, holy and pure unifications at all times. For this is the ultimate purpose of my existence: to bind together all the worlds, both spiritual and physical, and combine all Divine Names in absolute unity. In this way Your Oneness will be revealed and will shine forth to all creatures. "And they all will know You, from the least of them to the greatest of them."

I beseech You, my God and God of my ancestors, always be with me and protect me, that no harm result from any mystical unification I perform. Please rectify in Your mercy any harmful effects my past misdeeds have brought about in the mystical letter combinations of Your holy Names. Turn my sins into merits and nullify my evil acts, according to Your great goodness and wondrous kindness.

Deliver us in the merit of the *tzaddikim* who perform all supernal unifications to the highest degree of perfection and who reveal and make known to all humanity Your Oneness. In the merit of their holiness and righteousness, even our many transgressions will be completely nullified; our sins can actually be transformed to merits.

Master of the Universe, Who is One, Singular and Unique: have mercy upon us for Your Name's sake, and enable us to perceive You in truth. May we declare Your Name to all humanity, "that all the nations on earth may know that the Lord is God; nothing exists outside of Him."

(II:516–518)

HOSPITALITY

Master of the Universe, Kind and Merciful Father, help me acquire the holy trait of kindness. Like Abraham and Sarah, who performed deeds of kindness all their days, may I show hospitality to worthy guests, and may my house be a "gathering place for the wise." May I have guests who are *tzaddikim*, and may I receive them with great love, respect and joy. Grant me the privilege of personally attending to their needs and serving them in every way. May I humble myself completely before the wise, until I become a spiritual channel for the light of Abraham and Sarah, and so attain the trait of true kindness.

(I:425)

LOVE OF HUMANITY

Save me from all strife and conflict. May I harbor not even the slightest trace of negativity toward anything holy or toward any good person. Let me become a true vehicle for goodness and holiness. May I love and feel true affinity for every good person, every true *tzaddik* and all worthy beings in the world. Thus may I cleave to You, O God, and become merged within Your Oneness.

(I:644)

שלום

Shalom

Peace

A SONG OF PEACE

May we sing and play music in praise of God, until we become a channel for the melody that transcends all melodies, the Song of Songs, the song of King Solomon, the song of that man of peace, whose very name means "peace."

Bless us with Your peace, and bring peace to all your people—peace between friends and neighbors, peace between every husband and wife. May we never know hatred or jealousy, rivalry or discord. May this blessing of peace increase and spread forth to include all of humanity, until everyone is able to rouse his fellow to seek the truth, to contemplate the ultimate purpose of Creation, and not to waste his days in empty and meaningless pursuits. Then everyone will cast away the "false gods of silver and gold" and serve You in truth, with love and awe.

Bless us with peace, O God Who is exalted above all, and let us experience the prophecy of peace: "For you will go out with joy and will be led forth in peace; the mountains and the hills will burst into song before You, and all the trees of the field will clap hands." May the One Who makes peace in His heavens bring peace to us all.

(I:422–424)

PEACEFUL DIALOGUE

Master of peace, King unto Whom peace belongs: may it be Your will to bestow peace on Your people, Israel. Let peace abound and extend to all the inhabitants of the world until there is no longer any hatred, jealousy, conflict, strife or hostility between one person and another. May there be only great love and peace among all humanity. May we all recognize the love that others bear for us and know that they seek our good and our love, and that they desire our lasting success.

Then all people will be able to come together to engage in genuine dialogue and explain the truth to each other, inspiring one another to contemplate man's lot in this world. For this world passes as the blink of an eye, like a passing shadow—not even the shadow cast by a tree or a wall, but the shadow of a flying bird, which moves quickly out of view.

Let all people discuss with their friends the ultimate futility of worldly desires, and come to understand the true purpose of the soul's descent to this lowly world. Let us speak at length with each other in a spirit of brotherhood and love—truthfully, from the depths of our hearts, without any desire to win arguments or to provoke each other at all.

Through such dialogue may we all draw near to You in absolute sincerity, discarding our "false gods of silver and gold." May we cease to follow the crookedness of our hearts that draws us toward evil, and may we no longer waste our lives in the pursuit of wealth; may we neither chase after luxuries, nor seek to amass riches. Then the spirit of folly will be banished from our hearts, and peace will grow and spread throughout the world.

All Israel will return to You in complete repentance, as is Your beneficent will. All the nations of the world, too, will be aroused spiritually, and they will recognize the ultimate truth. They, too, will all draw near to You and accept upon themselves the yoke of Your Kingship, as the prophet has promised, "For I will turn the language of the nations to one of pure speech, that they all call upon the Name of God and serve Him with a common accord."

(1:409)

THE HIDDEN *TZADDIKIM*

Merciful God, reveal to us the hidden Torah (the "secrets" of Kabbalah) and the hidden *tzaddikim*. Even if the world does not yet deserve to glimpse this hidden light, deal with us mercifully; do not relate to us with strict justice. Arouse Your true mercy and kindness on our behalf, and help us to become worthy of the revelation of the hidden *tzaddikim* and the hidden Torah.

You know, O God, that we have no hope and nothing upon which to rely, except the hidden *tzaddikim* and the hidden Torah. Only they can protect us now, in the depths of this bitter exile, in the darkness that precedes the coming of the *Mashiach*. In Your mercy, awaken Your compassion, and help us to completely overcome the evil in our hearts, as You desire. May our deeds find favor in Your eyes, so that even in this world we may experience something of the supernal Light which is hidden and stored away for the *tzaddikim,* as the verses state, "Light is sown for the righteous and joy for the upright of heart," and, "Say of the righteous: It shall be well, for they shall eat the fruit of their deeds."

Send peace to the Jewish people; remove all strife from the world, until the influence of peace is so strong that those who have drifted far from You will be drawn near, to serve and revere You. Even those most distant from holiness, who are befouled by all sorts of abominations — may they all experience a spiritual awakening; may they draw near to You through the power of the true *tzaddikim,* who strive unremittingly to reveal Your Godliness and dominion to the Jewish people and to all of humanity.

Even in this world, let us taste of the wondrous peace that You shall reveal in Days to Come, as the prophet states, "And the wolf will dwell with the lamb, and the leopard will lie down with the kid, and the bull and the lion and the fattened calf together, and a small child shall lead them. They will do no harm, and they will destroy nothing in all My holy mountain; for the earth will be full of the knowledge of God as the waters cover the sea."

(I:497)

THE UNIVERSAL SHABBAT

May we receive the spirit of Shabbat with joy and gladness and with all our hearts.

Favor us, O God, and allow no worry or sorrow to disturb our day of rest. May we celebrate each Shabbat with true joy, with happiness and song, gladness and delight. Help us to draw the holiness of Shabbat into the days of the week, so that we may be joyous even then, delighting and rejoicing in You at all times.

Then God's absolute Oneness will be revealed to the world, so that everyone may know and believe that all diversity comes from the One Who is blessed and exalted forever. "And every living thing will know that You created it, and every entity will know that You formed it. And every being that has the breath of life in its nostrils will declare, 'The Lord, God of Israel, is King, and His dominion extends over all'."

O God, let Your Oneness be revealed to all through Your people, Israel, whom You have chosen as the "One Nation" to serve You from among all nations on the face of the earth. Just as Your Oneness is revealed to all humanity through Your holy people Israel, may Your Oneness be revealed above, in the spiritual worlds. Remove all conflict and strife forever, and bring us peace.

(II:58–59)

UNITY IN DIVERSITY

Master of peace, Who "makes peace and creates everything," help us always to hold fast to the Divine attribute of peace and make it our own. May there be absolute peace among all people, particularly between every husband and wife, without any trace of strife, even in the hidden depths of the heart. For You make peace at the loftiest levels, binding together even opposing forces such as fire and water in perfect unity, and in Your wondrous ways You make peace between them.

Thus, may You draw great peace upon us and upon everyone in the world, until all opposing views unite in great peace and love. May they combine to form one all-encompassing perception and one heart, in order to draw us near to You and Your Torah in truth. Then we will all join together in order to perform Your will wholeheartedly. God, Whose Name is "Peace," bless us with peace, and in this way confer upon us all blessings, all beneficial influences, and bring about our complete deliverance.

(I:967)

GOD'S LOVE

Help me always to recognize Your great love, O God. Your love is beyond measure or limit; nevertheless, You "constricted" Your Godliness and clothed Your love in the holy Torah and its precepts, which You lovingly revealed through Your faithful prophet Moses. Each of your precepts is a holy channel through which You may be perceived; through these holy pathways we may serve You in truth, with love and awe.

Have mercy upon me, and enable me to fulfill all of Your precepts with great love. Help me to sense the Divine love which emanates from the highest wisdom—the spiritual knowledge that one day will be revealed through the secrets of Torah, the "Torah of the Hidden Ancient One." This great love that existed before You created the world is a love that transcends time and space. Its light can be grasped only through the true *tzaddikim,* who have mastered their natural inclinations and have completely destroyed all their evil traits and desires. They alone rule their hearts, and can experience absolute love, without any trace of ego.

Help me to find and cleave to a true *tzaddik,* whose soul includes all souls, until my soul merges with the Universal Soul. For only a true *tzaddik* can reveal the Divine love that shines through the highest wisdom. In the merit and power of that *tzaddik,* may I too subjugate and destroy my evil inclination, so that I will be free of evil traits and desires. Open my heart to receive the light of wisdom, and let me succeed in binding all the traits of my heart to this knowledge. Thus may I realize that "Your Glory fills all the earth," and that everything is but a reflection of Your Oneness.

May my heart be illuminated with Divine wisdom, so that even within the diverse traits of the heart, even within the limitations of time, I will behold the "hidden light"—the Divine love that shines through the highest wisdom. Thus may I understand and intuitively grasp the secrets of Torah, constantly attaining higher levels of holy perception, constantly coming closer to You.

(I:495–496)

גאולה

Ge'ulah

Redemption

THE RETURN OF PROPHECY

"O God, give honor to Your people, praise to those who revere You, hope to those who seek You and confident speech to those who yearn for You." May our actions always bring You glory, and may Your glory spread throughout Creation. Then the spirit of prophecy, which left us on account of our sins, will be restored, in fulfillment of the verse, "And your sons and daughters will prophesy." Imbue us with holy wisdom, strength and wealth, until we all become worthy of receiving the spirit of prophecy and this world is made a dwelling place for the Divine Presence.

(II:194)

SONG OF REDEMPTION

O God and God of our ancestors, Who chose David and his descendants after him, and Who delights in songs of praise: in Your great mercy and kindness, recall the plight of the *Shekhinah*, Who has been driven from Her place like a bird driven from its nest. "Arise and have mercy upon Zion, for it is time to be gracious unto her, for the appointed time has come." Raise Israel from her fallen state; help us lift up our voices in song. Grant us the ability to offer You songs and praises with gladness and joy to make music all the days of our lives, sweet and pleasant music that God loves.

In Your great mercy, arouse the Jewish people to sing a song of gladness and rejoicing. Make it known throughout Creation, O God, that You alone rule over all Your works, so that the verse will be fulfilled:

"Sing, sing unto God; sing, sing unto our King, for God reigns over all the earth; sing, O enlightened one." Remember Your people, Israel, who are scattered among the nations, and Your Holy Temple, which lies forlorn and in ruins. "Even the bird has found a home, and the swallow a nest where she places her young, on the ruins of Your altars, O Lord of Hosts, my King and my God." Return the *Kohanim* (priests) to their Divine service, and the Levites to their place in the Holy Temple — return them to their songs and melodies; return Your people to their homeland. Grant us the holy wisdom and presence of mind to accept the yoke of Your kingship and to reveal Your sovereignty to all the world.

May You soon reestablish the throne of King David, and without a moment's delay bring the *Mashiach*, who is descended from David, the "sweet singer of Israel." "Then our mouths will be filled with gladness, and our tongues with joyous song." We will sing and make music before You, as the prophet has said, "We shall play musical instruments in God's Temple all the days of our lives."

(I:15, 18)

A NEW SONG

Merciful God, reveal Your Divine Providence throughout Creation. Renew the world in a way that everyone will know that all happenings reflect Divine Providence alone and not the dictates of nature.

Call forth a new song to the world, a song of wonders, as the Psalmist wrote: "Sing unto God a new song, for He has performed wonders." We will offer You our thanks with a new song for our redemption and for our spiritual deliverance. We will sing, chant and make music before You, creating new melodies, songs and praises, songs of wonders that transcend nature, until we experience the revelation of God's Essential Name. Then all of Creation will hear the song of a perfected world, the exalted song that emanates from the four letters of Your Essential Name; that song will be played on an instrument of seventy-two strings, in fulfillment of the verse "The world will be built through *chesed* (kindness)."

Master of the Universe: Grant me the gift of life, that I may live a true life and not perish, that I may experience the goodness of the World to Come. Be kind and gracious unto me, that I may hear the song of the future, when the time comes for Your world to be transformed and renewed.

Grant me the strength to shield my eyes and ears from the illusion that is this world, that I not gaze upon its vain allurements or hear its empty voice. Let me speak not even a single word that does not bring me closer to You and Your service. Thus will all my senses be purified so that they may serve as a channel for true song, in praise of Your great and holy Name.

Let me turn away from the materialism of this world and not breathe its air; let no breath of its illusion affect me. May my arms and legs be dedicated to Your service alone. My eyes and ears and mouth, my heart, my intellect and mind, my entire body with its 248 limbs and 365 tendons, and all my senses and abilities—may they all cleave to You in truth, with a firm and mighty bond, devoted to Your service forever.

Thus, may I merit to hear at last the holy and wondrous song of the future, that melody which will be played on the instrument of seventy-two strings. Fortunate are the ears that hear this song; fortunate are those who wait and long and yearn for this melody. "Fortunate is the one whom You choose and bring near," who merits to glimpse the circle of the *tzaddikim,* when the time arrives for them to experience this great and holy song for all eternity.

(II:200–201)

HIGHER THAN TIME

Master of the Universe, Who lives and endures forever: You are One before Creation and You are One after Creation, for Your Essence completely transcends time. All of time—whatever was and whatever shall be—amounts to not even so much as an instant before You.

In Your mercy grant me higher consciousness and true intellect, that I may be freed of the constraints of time and grasp the truth that time is an illusion. "Everything is but an empty breath, and our days are like a passing shadow." There is no concept of time for one who possesses true intellect; time exists only where wisdom is lacking. In Your wondrous and awesome ways You have concealed this higher form of wisdom from humanity, so that time seems to exist, all for the sake of free will. Yet in truth, only the "eternal present" is real.

Allow us to bind ourselves to the true *tzaddikim* who have succeeded in attaining this higher intellect, and so have transcended the constraints of time. They are saved from "the evil that takes place under the sun," the evil that can have an effect when one lives under the illusion of time. Help us to follow in their footsteps and go in their paths, heeding their spiritual advice and paying no attention to anything which comes under the dominion of time: all evil passions and negative character traits.

May I never become confused by the ups and downs of time. Rather, let me recall always the essential nonexistence of time—and let me bind myself to the dimension that transcends time, where all evil passions, negative character traits and confused thoughts are completely nullified.

(II:347)

FINDING ETERNITY
IN TIME

Enlighten us with holy wisdom, with the enlightenment of the *Mashiach*, of whom it is written: "I have given birth to you today." Then all evil and negativity will disappear, along with the illusion of time. We witness time racing and flowing, never stopping for a second; it cannot be grasped—because it does not really exist.

Spare us from the ravages of time; do not let us exchange eternal life for this illusory, transitory world. Grant us higher consciousness and true intellect, that we may perceive the insubstantial nature of time. Do not let us be fooled by the illusion of time.

May we begin anew to serve You, every day and every moment, and may we never be thrown off course by anything that happened in the past.

Let us sanctify ourselves in truth and thereby

incorporate time into the dimension that is higher than time. In this way we can entirely transcend the limits of time and space, for that is Your will and the will of the true *tzaddikim* who have fully attained this level. "Return to us, O God, and we shall return to You; renew our days as before"—before the creation of time.

(II:349)

THE JOY OF REDEMPTION

May our thoughts stream always toward the perception of the Infinite Light, toward the highest spiritual level, in great holiness and purity, in truth and in perfect faith. Awaken Your mercies upon us, and hasten the Final Redemption. Restore us from our state of devastation and ruin, and rebuild Your Holy Temple. Repair all the palaces of holiness, both the physical and the spiritual, and cause us to feel gladness always. Lift up the *Shekhinah* from Her exile among the *kelipot* (powers of evil), from Her imprisonment in the Realm of Unholiness.

Extricate all the sparks of holiness; overthrow, subjugate and destroy all the powers of evil and forces of the Other Side. "They will all bow down and prostrate themselves, and they will give honor to the glory of Your Name."

Bring us speedily out of exile, both our physical and spiritual exile, with great joy. Then all nations will respectfully defer to Israel and seek its benefit, for they will clearly perceive the holiness of the Jewish people, whom God has chosen. As the verse states, "They will bring all your brothers from all the nations on horses and in chariots, in wagons and upon mules and camels, as a tribute to God on My holy mountain, Jerusalem, says the Lord, just as the Children of Israel bring an offering in a pure vessel to God's House."

Then joy will spread through all the world, as it is written, "For with joy you will go forth and be led in peace; the mountains and hills will burst into song before you, and all the trees of the field will clap hands. For God has consoled Zion, consoled all of her ruins. He has made her wilderness like Eden and her desert like the Garden of the Lord. Gladness and rejoicing will flourish there, thanksgiving and song."

(1:396)

Notes

How to Use This Book
1. *Berakhot,* 4:4
2. *Likutey Tefilot,* Introduction
3. *Tzava'at HaRivash* 7

About These Prayers
1. *Yemey Moharnat,* I:1
2. *Chayey Moharan* 2, also note *Parparaot L'Chokhmah* 6:15
3. Exodus 33:11
4. *Chayey Moharan* 367
5. For a full biography of Reb Noson, see *Through Fire And Water,* by Chaim Kramer, published by the Breslov Research Institute.
6. See *Likutey Halakhot, Shluchin* 5; *Chayey Moharan* 46, 196, 218, 229, 322, 373; *Parparaot L'Chokhmah* 61:8; *Tzion Hamtzuyenet* 78.
7. cf. *Likutey Moharan* II:100
8. *Likutey Moharan* I:52

9. *Tzava'at HaRivash* 41
10. *Pisgamin Kaddishin* 17a, citing R. Aharon of Zhitomir
11. *Keter Shem Tov* 216
12. See *Through Fire And Water*, Ch. 25, esp. note 2, p. 612. Another collection of original Kabbalistic prayers that was popular among the devout in Rebbe Nachman's day, and remains so, is the *Sha'arey Zion* of the sixteenth-century mystic, Rabbi Noson Hanover. Also, the Yiddish *Techinot* (Supplications) commonly recited in Eastern Europe were praised by Rebbe Nachman (*Sichot HaRan* 10). Some of these *Techinot* have been rendered into English in recent years, inspiring another generation of Jews in America.
13. cf. *Likutey Tefilot*, Introduction
14. *Likutey Moharan* II:25, et al.
15. *Through Fire And Water*, Ch. 31, 45
16. *Likutey Moharan* I:24
17. *Ibid*. 22:9–10
18. *Chayey Moharan* 254, 392

Glossary

Amidah: The silent prayer of eighteen blessings recited while standing.

Chasid/Chasidim: Literally, "devout"; a member of the mystical/pietist movement founded by the Baal Shem Tov (Rabbi Yisrael Ben Eliezer) in mid-eighteenth century.

Chesed: Literally, "lovingkindness." The numerical value of the Hebrew word *chesed* is seventy-two, thus the "Song of the Future"—the lovingkindness that God will reveal—will be the music played on a harp of "seventy-two" strings.

Daven/Davening (Yid.): To pray/prayer.

Deveykut: Literally, "cleaving"; spiritual communion with God.

Four Worlds: The Kabbalah describes four "worlds"

or levels of reality: *Atzilut* (Emanation) is the World of Oneness; *Beriyah* (Creation) is the World of the Divine Throne; *Yetzirah* (Formation) is the world of the angels; *Asiyah* (Action) encompasses the entire physical universe.

Halakhah: Jewish religious law.

Hitbodedut: Literally, "seclusion"; more commonly known as *hisbodedus*. In Breslov Chasidut, an approach to meditation and spontaneous personal prayer recommended by Rebbe Nachman, ideally practiced in fields or forest at night. (*Outpouring of the Soul*, available from the Breslov Research Institute, presents Rebbe Nachman's path of meditation and *hitbodedut*.)

Kabbalah: "That which can be received"; the Jewish mystical tradition.

Kelipot: Literally, "husks." In Kabbalistic literature, the spiritual disharmony of the universe is characterized by "sparks" of holiness descending into a state of exile from their Divine Source and becoming occluded by the *kelipot* that conceal the true nature of reality.

Manhig: Leader; in the Breslover Chasidic community, the senior disciple to whom others may turn for spiritual instruction or advice.

Mashiach: The Messiah

Minyan: Prayer quorum of ten men.

Mitzvah/Mitzvot: Religious commandment or precept.

Nefesh: A part of the soul. *Nefesh* is the "lower soul" that enlivens the body. The transcendent levels of the soul are known as *Chayah* and *Yechidah*.

Neshamah: A part of the soul. *Neshamah* is the "human soul" that is the seat of intellect. See also *Nefesh*.

Rebbe (Yid.): A rabbi or teacher, especially a Chasidic leader.

Ruach: A part of the soul. *Ruach* is the "spirit" that is the seat of the emotions. See also *Nefesh*.

Shabbat: The seventh day, one of rest, that commemorates the Divine act of Creation.

Shekhinah: The Divine Presence.

Torah: The Five Books of Moses; more generally, Jewish religious law and literature.

Talmud: The authoritative discussions and interpretations of Torah law, as well as the wisdom of the Sages of Israel, redacted approximately 500 C.E. by Ravina and Rav Ashi.

Tzaddik/Tzaddikim: Literally, "righteous"; in Chasidic thought, one who has perfected his soul and is capable of elevating others from their confusion and inner obstacles, enabling them ultimately to perceive Godliness.

Index

NOTES

NOTES

About the Breslov Research Institute

Rebbe Nachman was only thirty-eight years old when he passed away in 1810. Yet, shortly before his passing, he told his followers that his influence would endure long afterwards. "My light will burn until the days of the Mashiach [Messiah]." Generations of readers have been enthralled and inspired by his writings, which have been explored and interpreted by leading scholars around the globe.

The growing interest in Rebbe Nachman from all sectors—academia and laymen alike—led to the establishment of the Breslov Research Institute in Jerusalem in 1979. Since then a team of scholars has been engaged in research into the texts, oral traditions and music of the Breslov movement. The purpose of the Institute is to publish authoritative translations, commentaries and general works on Breslov Chassidut. Projects also include the recording of Breslov songs and melodies on cassette and in music book form.

Offices and representatives of the Breslov Research Institute:

Israel:

Breslov Research Institute
P.O. Box 5370
Jerusalem, Israel
Tel: (011-9722) 582-4641
Fax: (011-9722) 582-5542
www.breslov.org

North America:

Breslov Research Institute
P.O. Box 587
Monsey, NY 10952-0587
Tel: (845) 425-4258
Fax: (845) 425-3018
www.breslov.org

Breslov books may be ordered directly from these offices.

BRESLOV RESEARCH INSTITUTE BOOKS

Rabbi Nachman's Stories
Translated by *Rabbi Aryeh Kaplan*

The Sages always told stories to convey some of the deepest secrets about God and His relation to the creation. Rebbe Nachman developed this ancient art to perfection. Spellbinding and entertaining, these stories are fast moving, richly structured and filled with penetrating insights. Rabbi Kaplan's translation is accompanied by a masterful commentary drawn from the works of Rebbe Nachman's chassidim.

6 x 9, 552 pages, HC, Bibliography, Index, ISBN 0-930213-02-5 **$21.00**

Crossing the Narrow Bridge
A Practical Guide to Rebbe Nachman's Teachings
by *Chaim Kramer*; ed. by *Moshe Mykoff*

Rebbe Nachman taught: "The world is a very narrow bridge. The main thing is not to be afraid." Lively, down to earth and easy to read, this book provides clear, detailed guidance in how to apply Rebbe Nachman's teachings in modern everyday life. Subjects include faith, joy, meditating, earning a living, health, raising children, etc., and provide a wealth of anecdotes from the lives of leading Breslov chassidim.

5½ x 8½, 452 pages, HC, Appendices, ISBN 0-930213-40-8 **$17.00**

The Breslov Haggadah
Compiled and translated by *Rabbi Yehoshua Starret* and *Chaim Kramer*; ed. by *Moshe Mykoff*

The classic Pesach Haggadah accompanied by Rebbe Nachman's unique insights and other commentary material drawn from Breslov and general sources. Includes appendices on: The Story of Exodus, Pesach Anecdotes, Chassidic insights into *Sefirat HaOmer, Chol HaMoed,* and *Shavuot.* 6½ x 9½, 256 pages, HC, Appendices, ISBN 0-930213-35-1 **$16.00**

Esther: *A Breslov Commentary on the Megillah*
Compiled and adapted by *Rabbi Yehoshua Starret*; ed. by *Ozer Bergman*

Insights from Rebbe Nachman and his followers that "unmask" the Megillah's deeper meaning in the modern context and for each of us personally. Includes Hebrew text of the Megillah, laws of the holiday and historical overview.
6 x 8½, 160 pages, PB, Appendices, ISBN 0-930213-42-4 **$12.00**

Chanukah—*With Rebbe Nachman of Breslov*
Compiled and adapted by *Rabbi Yehoshua Starret*

Traces the historical roots—and spiritual implications—of the Chanukah story, and provides deeper insight into the holiday's laws and their meaning for today. Based on the timeless wisdom of Rebbe Nachman and other Chassidic masters, this work lights the way on the journey from ancient Israel to the future, and into the mind and heart.
5 x 8, 128 pages, PB, ISBN 0-930213-99-8 **$10.00**

Garden of the Souls: *Rebbe Nachman on Suffering*
by *Avraham Greenbaum*

Offers guidance and comfort in dealing with pain and suffering in our own lives and those of the people around us. Faith makes it possible to find meaning in the trials of this world and turn them into experiences that can elevate us spiritually and open us to profound joy.
5 x 8, 96 pages, PB, ISBN 0-930213-39-4 **$8.00**

Anatomy of the Soul
by *Chaim Kramer*; ed. by *Avraham Sutton*

Explores the mystical meaning of the teaching that human beings are created in the image of God; provides an in-depth study of how the different systems of the human body relate to the ten *sefirot* and the five levels of the soul, and how through the body's organs and limbs we influence the hidden spiritual universes.
6 x 9, 364 pages, HC, Appendices, ISBN 0-930213-51-3 **$20.00**

Rabbi Nachman's Wisdom
Translated by *Rabbi Aryeh Kaplan*; ed. by *Rabbi Zvi Aryeh Rosenfeld*

A classic collection of Rebbe Nachman's conversations and teachings, ranging from comments on everyday practical topics to fundamental insights about faith and Jewish mysticism. The conversations provide a vivid picture of the Master, his wit, directness and wisdom. Also included is an account of Rebbe Nachman's adventure-filled pilgrimage to the Holy Land at the height of Napoleon's campaign in the Middle East in 1798.
6 x 9, 486 pages, HC, Appendices, Index, ISBN 0-930213-00-9 **$16.00**

Likutey Moharan: *The Collected Teachings of Rabbi Nachman*
Translated by *Moshe Mykoff*; annotated by *Chaim Kramer*

The first authoritative translation of Rebbe Nachman's *magnum opus*, presented with facing punctuated Hebrew text, full explanatory notes, source references and supplementary information relating to the lessons. Each volume is accompanied by appendices and charts clarifying pertinent kabbalistic concepts; the first volume includes Reb Noson's introduction to the original work, short biographies of leading Breslov personalities and a bibliography.
Vol. 1—*Lessons 1–6:* 6½ x 9½, HC, ISBN 0-930213-92-0 **$20.00**
Vol. 2—*Lessons 7–16:* 6½ x 9½, HC, ISBN 0-930213-93-9 **$20.00**
Vol. 3—*Lessons 17–22:* 6½ x 9½, HC, ISBN 0-930213-78-5 **$20.00**
Vol. 4—*Lessons 23–32:* 6½ x 9½, HC, ISBN 0-930213-79-3 **$20.00**
Vol. 5—*Lessons 33–48:* 6½ x 9½, HC, ISBN 0-930213-80-7 **$20.00**
Vol. 6—*Lessons 49–57:* 6½ x 9½, HC, ISBN 0-930213-81-5 **$20.00**
Vol. 7—*Lessons 58–64:* 6½ x 9½, HC, ISBN 0-930213-82-3 **$20.00**
Vol. 8—*Lessons 65–72:* 6½ x 9½, HC, ISBN 0-930213-88-8 **$20.00**
Vol. 10—*Lessons 109–194:* 6½ x 9½, HC, ISBN 0-930213-85-8 **$20.00**
Vol. 11—*Lessons 195–286:* 6½ x 9½, HC, ISBN 0-930213-86-6 **$20.00**

Until the Mashiach

by *Rabbi Aryeh Kaplan*; ed. by *Rabbi Dovid Shapiro*

A scholarly research work that presents the events of Rebbe Nachman's life in a chronological format, with full source references throughout. Features an extensive historical overview, detailed maps and full appendices covering significant towns and cities, biographical information and anecdotes about Rebbe Nachman's family, pupils and other contemporary figures, his letters, a comprehensive family tree, and more.

6 x 9, 379 pages, HC, Appendices, Index, ISBN 0-930213-08-4 **$16.00**

Explorations: *A Mini-Series of Rebbe Nachman's Lessons*

Azamra—I Will Sing

Explores the way to happiness by finding the good in ourselves and in others.

4½ x 6½, 64 pages, PB, ISBN 0-930213-11-4 **$3.00**

Tsohar—Light

Explores the way through life's worst entanglement by shining the light of truth into all situations.

4½ x 6½, 64 pages, PB, ISBN 0-930213-26-2 **$3.00**

Mayim—Water

Explores free will based on the Talmudic teaching about the four who entered paradise.

4½ x 6½, 64 pages, PB, ISBN 0-930213-28-9 **$3.00**

Ayeh?—Where?

Explores how to find hope in even the darkest situations and turn them to one's advantage.

4½ x 6½, 64 pages, PB, ISBN 0-930213-12-2 **$3.00**

The Breslov Music Book: *Shabbat—Azamer Bishvochin (vol. 1)*

by *Ben-Zion Solomon*

The traditional music of the Breslov chassidim for Shabbat night prayers and meal, transcribed (with chords). Fully researched and annotated, includes history of each tune, vocalized Hebrew, facing English translation and transliteration.

8 x 11, 125 pages, PB, Spiral binding, ISBN 0-930213-36-X **$20.00**

The Breslov Music Book: *Shabbat—Asader LiS'udoso (vol. 2)*

by *Ben-Zion Solomon*

The traditional music of the Breslov chassidim for Shabbat morning prayers and the morning and afternoon meals, transcribed (with chords). Fully researched and annotated, includes history of each tune, vocalized Hebrew, facing English translation and transliteration. 8 x 11, 125 pages, PB, Spiral binding, ISBN 0-930213-60-2 **$20.00**

Audio Cassettes and CDs

Full-scale production of favorite Breslov Shabbat songs including some of Rebbe Nachman's own melodies. Cassettes **$12.00** each; CDs **$20.00** each.

Azamer Bishvochin—songs of the Shabbat evening prayers and the first meal

Me'eyn Olom Habo—songs of the first meal and the Shabbat morning prayers

Asader LiS'udoso—songs of the second Shabbat meal

B'nei Heicholo—songs of the third Shabbat meal

Bar/Bat Mitzvah

The JGirl's Guide: The Young Jewish Woman's Handbook for Coming of Age
By Penina Adelman, Ali Feldman, and Shulamit Reinharz
An inspirational, interactive guidebook designed to help pre-teen Jewish girls address the spiritual, educational, and psychological issues surrounding coming of age in today's society.   6 x 9, 240 pp, Quality PB, ISBN 1-58023-215-9 **$14.99**
Also Available: **The JGirl's Teacher's and Parent's Guide**
8½ x 11, 56 pp, PB, ISBN 1-58023-225-6 **$8.99**

Bar/Bat Mitzvah Basics: A Practical Family Guide to Coming of Age Together
By Helen Leneman   6 x 9, 240 pp, Quality PB, ISBN 1-58023-151-9 **$18.95**

The Bar/Bat Mitzvah Memory Book: An Album for Treasuring the Spiritual Celebration
By Rabbi Jeffrey K. Salkin and Nina Salkin
8 x 10, 48 pp, Deluxe Hardcover, 2-color text, ribbon marker, ISBN 1-58023-111-X **$19.95**

For Kids—Putting God on Your Guest List: How to Claim the Spiritual Meaning of Your Bar or Bat Mitzvah *By Rabbi Jeffrey K. Salkin*
6 x 9, 144 pp, Quality PB, ISBN 1-58023-015-6 **$14.99** *For ages 11–12*

Putting God on the Guest List, 3rd Edition: How to Reclaim the Spiritual Meaning of Your Child's Bar or Bat Mitzvah *By Rabbi Jeffrey K. Salkin*
6 x 9, 224 pp, Quality PB, ISBN 1-58023-222-1 **$16.99**; Hardcover, ISBN 1-58023-260-4 **$24.99**
Also Available: **Putting God on the Guest List Teacher's Guide**
8½ x 11, 48 pp, PB, ISBN 1-58023-226-4 **$8.99**

Tough Questions Jews Ask: A Young Adult's Guide to Building a Jewish Life
By Rabbi Edward Feinstein 6 x 9, 160 pp, Quality PB, ISBN 1-58023-139-X **$14.99** *For ages 13 & up*
Also Available: **Tough Questions Jews Ask Teacher's Guide**
8½ x 11, 72 pp, PB, ISBN 1-58023-187-X **$8.95**

Bible Study/Midrash

Hineini in Our Lives: Learning How to Respond to Others through 14 Biblical Texts, and Personal Stories *By Norman J. Cohen* 6 x 9, 240 pp, Hardcover, ISBN 1-58023-131-4 **$23.95**

Ancient Secrets: Using the Stories of the Bible to Improve Our Everyday Lives
By Rabbi Levi Meier, Ph.D. 5½ x 8½, 288 pp, Quality PB, ISBN 1-58023-064-4 **$16.95**

Moses—The Prince, the Prophet: His Life, Legend & Message for Our Lives
By Rabbi Levi Meier, Ph.D.   6 x 9, 224 pp, Quality PB, ISBN 1-58023-069-5 **$16.95**

Self, Struggle & Change: Family Conflict Stories in Genesis and Their Healing Insights for Our Lives *By Norman J. Cohen*   6 x 9, 224 pp, Quality PB, ISBN 1-879045-66-4 **$18.99**

Voices from Genesis: Guiding Us through the Stages of Life *By Norman J. Cohen*
6 x 9, 192 pp, Quality PB, ISBN 1-58023-118-7 **$16.95**

Congregation Resources

Becoming a Congregation of Learners: Learning as a Key to Revitalizing Congregational Life *By Isa Aron, Ph.D. Foreword by Rabbi Lawrence A. Hoffman.*
6 x 9, 304 pp, Quality PB, ISBN 1-58023-089-X **$19.95**

Finding a Spiritual Home: How a New Generation of Jews Can Transform the American Synagogue *By Rabbi Sidney Schwarz*
6 x 9, 352 pp, Quality PB, ISBN 1-58023-185-3 **$19.95**

The Self-Renewing Congregation: Organizational Strategies for Revitalizing Congregational Life *By Isa Aron, Ph.D. Foreword by Dr. Ron Wolfson.*
6 x 9, 304 pp, Quality PB, ISBN 1-58023-166-7 **$19.95**

Or phone, fax, mail or e-mail to: **JEWISH LIGHTS** Publishing
Sunset Farm Offices, Route 4 • P.O. Box 237 • Woodstock, Vermont 05091
Tel: (802) 457-4000 • Fax: (802) 457-4004 • www.jewishlights.com
Credit card orders: (800) 962-4544 (8:30AM–5:30PM ET Monday–Friday)
Generous discounts on quantity orders. SATISFACTION GUARANTEED. Prices subject to change.

Current Events/History

The Story of the Jews: A 4,000-Year Adventure—A Graphic History Book
Written & illustrated by Stan Mack
Witty, illustrated narrative of all the major happenings from biblical times to the twenty-first century. 6 x 9, 288 pp, illus., Quality PB, ISBN 1-58023-155-1 **$16.95**

Hannah Senesh: Her Life and Diary, the First Complete Edition
By Hannah Senesh; Foreword by Marge Piercy; Preface by Eitan Senesh
6 x 9, 352 pp, Hardcover, ISBN 1-58023-212-4 **$24.99**

The Jewish Prophet: Visionary Words from Moses and Miriam to Henrietta Szold and A. J. Heschel *By Rabbi Michael J. Shire*
6½ x 8½, 128 pp, 123 full-color illus., Hardcover, ISBN 1-58023-168-3 **Special gift price $14.95**

Shared Dreams: Martin Luther King, Jr. & the Jewish Community
By Rabbi Marc Schneier. Preface by Martin Luther King III.
6 x 9, 240 pp, Hardcover, ISBN 1-58023-062-8 **$24.95**

"Who Is a Jew?": Conversations, Not Conclusions *By Meryl Hyman*
6 x 9, 272 pp, Quality PB, ISBN 1-58023-052-0 **$16.95**

Ecology

Ecology & the Jewish Spirit: Where Nature & the Sacred Meet
Edited by Ellen Bernstein 6 x 9, 288 pp, Quality PB, ISBN 1-58023-082-2 **$16.95**

Torah of the Earth: Exploring 4,000 Years of Ecology in Jewish Thought
Vol. 1: Biblical Israel: One Land, One People; Rabbinic Judaism: One People, Many Lands
Vol. 2: Zionism: One Land, Two Peoples; Eco-Judaism: One Earth, Many Peoples
Edited by Rabbi Arthur Waskow
Vol. 1: 6 x 9, 272 pp, Quality PB, ISBN 1-58023-086-5 **$19.95**
Vol. 2: 6 x 9, 336 pp, Quality PB, ISBN 1-58023-087-3 **$19.95**

The Way Into Judaism and the Environment
By Jeremy Benstein, PhD
6 x 9, 225 pp (est.), Hardcover, ISBN 1-58023-268-X **$24.99**

Grief/Healing

Against the Dying of the Light: A Parent's Story of Love, Loss and Hope
By Leonard Fein
5½ x 8½, 176 pp, Quality PB, ISBN 1-58023-197-7 **$15.99**; Hardcover, ISBN 1-58023-110-1 **$19.95**

Grief in Our Seasons: A Mourner's Kaddish Companion *By Rabbi Kerry M. Olitzky*
4½ x 6½, 448 pp, Quality PB, ISBN 1-879045-55-9 **$15.95**

Healing of Soul, Healing of Body: Spiritual Leaders Unfold the Strength & Solace in Psalms *Edited by Rabbi Simkha Y. Weintraub, C.S.W.*
6 x 9, 128 pp, 2-color illus. text, Quality PB, ISBN 1-879045-31-1 **$14.99**

Jewish Paths toward Healing and Wholeness: A Personal Guide to Dealing with Suffering *By Rabbi Kerry M. Olitzky. Foreword by Debbie Friedman.*
6 x 9, 192 pp, Quality PB, ISBN 1-58023-068-7 **$15.95**

Mourning & Mitzvah, 2nd Edition: A Guided Journal for Walking the Mourner's Path through Grief to Healing *By Anne Brener, L.C.S.W.*
7½ x 9, 304 pp, Quality PB, ISBN 1-58023-113-6 **$19.95**

The Perfect Stranger's Guide to Funerals and Grieving Practices
A Guide to Etiquette in Other People's Religious Ceremonies *Edited by Stuart M. Matlins*
6 x 9, 240 pp, Quality PB, ISBN 1-893361-20-9 **$16.95** *(A SkyLight Paths book)*

A Time to Mourn, A Time to Comfort, 2nd Edition: A Guide to Jewish Bereavement and Comfort *By Dr. Ron Wolfson*
7 x 9, 336 pp, Quality PB, ISBN 1-58023-253-1 **$19.99**

When a Grandparent Dies: A Kid's Own Remembering Workbook for Dealing with Shiva and the Year Beyond *By Nechama Liss-Levinson, Ph.D.*
8 x 10, 48 pp, 2-color text, Hardcover, ISBN 1-879045-44-3 **$15.95** *For ages 7–13*

Abraham Joshua Heschel

The Earth Is the Lord's: The Inner World of the Jew in Eastern Europe
5½ x 8, 128 pp, Quality PB, ISBN 1-879045-42-7 **$14.95**

Israel: An Echo of Eternity *New Introduction by Susannah Heschel*
5½ x 8, 272 pp, Quality PB, ISBN 1-879045-70-2 **$19.95**

A Passion for Truth: Despair and Hope in Hasidism
5½ x 8, 352 pp, Quality PB, ISBN 1-879045-41-9 **$18.99**

Holidays/Holy Days

Rosh Hashanah Readings: Inspiration, Information and Contemplation
Edited by Rabbi Dov Peretz Elkins with section introductions from Arthur Green's These Are the Words
A powerful collection of writings about Rosh Hashanah that will add spiritual depth and holiness to your experience of the Jewish New Year.
6 x 9, 350 pp (est), Hardcover, ISBN 1-58023-239-6 **$24.99** Available June '06.

Yom Kippur Readings: Inspiration, Information and Contemplation
Edited by Rabbi Dov Peretz Elkins with section introductions from Arthur Green's These Are the Words
An extraordinary collection of readings, prayers and insights that enable the modern worshiper to enter into the spirit of the Day of Atonement in a personal and powerful way, permitting the meaning of Yom Kippur to enter the heart.
6 x 9, 348 pp, Hardcover, ISBN 1-58023-271-X **$24.99**

Leading the Passover Journey
The Seder's Meaning Revealed, the Haggadah's Story Retold
By Rabbi Nathan Laufer
Uncovers the hidden meaning of the Seder's rituals and customs
6 x 9, 208 pp, Hardcover, ISBN 1-58023-211-6 **$24.99**

7th Heaven: Celebrating Shabbat with Rebbe Nachman of Breslov
By Moshe Mykoff with the Breslov Research Institute
Explores the art of consciously observing Shabbat and understanding in-depth many of the day's spiritual practices. 5⅛ x 8¼, 224 pp, Deluxe PB w/flaps, ISBN 1-58023-175-6 **$18.95**

Creating Lively Passover Seders: A Sourcebook of Engaging Tales, Texts & Activities
By David Arnow, Ph.D. 7 x 9, 416 pp, Quality PB, ISBN 1-58023-184-5 **$24.99**

Hanukkah, 2nd Edition: The Family Guide to Spiritual Celebration
By Dr. Ron Wolfson. Edited by Joel Lurie Grishaver.
7 x 9, 240 pp, illus., Quality PB, ISBN 1-58023-122-5 **$18.95**

The Jewish Family Fun Book: Holiday Projects, Everyday Activities, and Travel Ideas
with Jewish Themes *By Danielle Dardashti and Roni Sarig. Illus. by Avi Katz.*
6 x 9, 288 pp, 70+ b/w illus. & diagrams, Quality PB, ISBN 1-58023-171-3 **$18.95**

The Jewish Gardening Cookbook: Growing Plants & Cooking for
Holidays & Festivals *By Michael Brown* 6 x 9, 224 pp, 30+ illus., Quality PB, ISBN 1-58023-116-0 **$16.95**

The Jewish Lights Book of Fun Classroom Activities: Simple and Seasonal
Projects for Teachers and Students *By Danielle Dardashti and Roni Sarig*
6 x 9, 240 pp, Quality PB, ISBN 1-58023-206-X **$19.99**

Passover, 2nd Edition: The Family Guide to Spiritual Celebration
By Dr. Ron Wolfson with Joel Lurie Grishaver 7 x 9, 352 pp, Quality PB, ISBN 1-58023-174-8
$19.95

Shabbat, 2nd Edition: The Family Guide to Preparing for and Celebrating the Sabbath
By Dr. Ron Wolfson 7 x 9, 320 pp, illus., Quality PB, ISBN 1-58023-164-0 **$19.95**

Sharing Blessings: Children's Stories for Exploring the Spirit of the Jewish Holidays
By Rahel Musleah and Michael Klayman
8½ x 11, 64 pp, Full-color illus., Hardcover, ISBN 1-879045-71-0 **$18.95** *For ages 6 & up*

Inspiration

God in All Moments
Mystical & Practical Spiritual Wisdom from Hasidic Masters
Edited and translated by Or N. Rose with Ebn D. Leader
Hasidic teachings on how to be mindful in religious practice and cultivating everyday ethical behavior—*hanhagot.* 5½ x 8½, 192 pp, Quality PB, ISBN 1-58023-186-1 **$16.95**

Our Dance with God: Finding Prayer, Perspective and Meaning in the Stories of Our Lives *By Karyn D. Kedar*
Inspiring spiritual insight to guide you on your life journeys and teach you to live and thrive in two conflicting worlds: the rational/material and the spiritual.
6 x 9, 176 pp, Quality PB, ISBN 1-58023-202-7 **$16.99**

Also Available: **The Dance of the Dolphin** (Hardcover edition of *Our Dance with God*)
6 x 9, 176 pp, Hardcover, ISBN 1-58023-154-3 **$19.95**

The Empty Chair: Finding Hope and Joy—Timeless Wisdom from a Hasidic Master, Rebbe Nachman of Breslov *Adapted by Moshe Mykoff and the Breslov Research Institute*
4 x 6, 128 pp, 2-color text, Deluxe PB w/flaps, ISBN 1-879045-67-2 **$9.95**

The Gentle Weapon: Prayers for Everyday and Not-So-Everyday Moments— Timeless Wisdom from the Teachings of the Hasidic Master, Rebbe Nachman of Breslov *Adapted by Moshe Mykoff and S. C. Mizrahi, together with the Breslov Research Institute*
4 x 6, 144 pp, 2-color text, Deluxe PB w/flaps, ISBN 1-58023-022-9 **$9.95**

God Whispers: Stories of the Soul, Lessons of the Heart *By Karyn D. Kedar*
6 x 9, 176 pp, Quality PB, ISBN 1-58023-088-1 **$15.95**

An Orphan in History: One Man's Triumphant Search for His Jewish Roots
By Paul Cowan. Afterword by Rachel Cowan. 6 x 9, 288 pp, Quality PB, ISBN 1-58023-135-7 **$16.95**

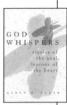

Kabbalah/Mysticism/Enneagram

Awakening to Kabbalah: The Guiding Light of Spiritual Fulfillment
By Rav Michael Laitman, PhD
A distinctive, personal and awe-filled introduction to this ancient wisdom tradition.
6 x 9, 192 pp, Hardcover, ISBN 1-58023-264-7 **$21.99**

Seek My Face: A Jewish Mystical Theology
By Dr. Arthur Green
This classic work of contemporary Jewish theology, revised and updated, is a profound, deeply personal statement of the lasting truths of Jewish mysticism and the basic faith claims of Judaism. 6 x 9, 304 pp, Quality PB, ISBN 1-58023-130-6 **$19.95**

Zohar: Annotated & Explained
Translation and annotation by Dr. Daniel C. Matt. Foreword by Andrew Harvey
Offers insightful yet unobtrusive commentary to the masterpiece of Jewish mysticism. 5½ x 8½, 160 pp, Quality PB, ISBN 1-893361-51-9 **$15.99** *(A SkyLight Paths book)*

Cast in God's Image: Discover Your Personality Type Using the Enneagram and Kabbalah
By Rabbi Howard A. Addison
7 x 9, 176 pp, Quality PB, Layflat binding, 20+ journaling exercises, ISBN 1-58023-124-1 **$16.95**

Ehyeh: A Kabbalah for Tomorrow *By Dr. Arthur Green*
6 x 9, 224 pp, Quality PB, ISBN 1-58023-213-2 **$16.99;** Hardcover, ISBN 1-58023-125-X **$21.95**

The Enneagram and Kabbalah: Reading Your Soul, 2nd Edition *By Rabbi Howard A. Addison*
6 x 9, 192 pp, Quality PB, ISBN 1-58023-229-9 **$16.99**

Finding Joy: A Practical Spiritual Guide to Happiness *By Dannel I. Schwartz with Mark Hass*
6 x 9, 192 pp, Quality PB, ISBN 1-58023-009-1 **$14.95**

The Gift of Kabbalah: Discovering the Secrets of Heaven, Renewing Your Life on Earth
By Tamar Frankiel, Ph.D.
6 x 9, 256 pp, Quality PB, ISBN 1-58023-141-1 **$16.95;** Hardcover, ISBN 1-58023-108-X **$21.95**

The Way Into Jewish Mystical Tradition *By Lawrence Kushner*
6 x 9, 224 pp, Quality PB, ISBN 1-58023-200-0 **$18.99;** Hardcover, ISBN 1-58023-029-6 **$21.95**

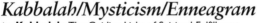

Life Cycle
Marriage / Parenting / Family / Aging

Jewish Fathers: A Legacy of Love
Photographs by Lloyd Wolf. Essays by Paula Wolfson. Foreword by Harold S. Kushner.
Honors the role of contemporary Jewish fathers in America. Each father tells in his own words what it means to be a parent and Jewish, and what he learned from his own father. Insightful photos. 9½ x 9⅞, 144 pp with 100+ duotone photos, Hardcover, ISBN 1-58023-204-3 **$30.00**

The Jewish Pregnancy Book: A Resource for the Soul, Body & Mind during Pregnancy, Birth & the First Three Months
By Sandy Falk, M.D., and Rabbi Daniel Judson, with Steven A. Rapp
Includes medical information, prayers and rituals for each stage of pregnancy, from a liberal Jewish perspective. 7 x 10, 208 pp, Quality PB, b/w illus., ISBN 1-58023-178-0 **$16.95**

Celebrating Your New Jewish Daughter: Creating Jewish Ways to Welcome Baby Girls into the Covenant—New and Traditional Ceremonies
By Debra Nussbaum Cohen 6 x 9, 272 pp, Quality PB, ISBN 1-58023-090-3 **$18.95**

The New Jewish Baby Book, 2nd Edition: Names, Ceremonies & Customs—A Guide for Today's Families *By Anita Diamant* 6 x 9, 336 pp, Quality PB, ISBN 1-58023-251-5 **$19.99**

The Creative Jewish Wedding Book: A Hands-On Guide to New & Old Traditions, Ceremonies & Celebrations *By Gabrielle Kaplan-Mayer*
Provides the tools to create the most meaningful Jewish traditional or alternative wedding by using ritual elements to express your unique style and spirituality. 9 x 9, 288 pp, b/w photos, Quality PB, ISBN 1-58023-194-2 **$19.99**

A Heart of Wisdom: Making the Jewish Journey from Midlife through the Elder Years
Edited by Susan Berrin. Foreword by Harold Kushner. 6 x 9, 384 pp, Quality PB, ISBN 1-58023-051-2 **$18.95**

So That Your Values Live On: Ethical Wills and How to Prepare Them
Edited by Jack Riemer and Nathaniel Stampfer
6 x 9, 272 pp, Quality PB, ISBN 1-879045-34-6 **$18.95**

Travel—Israel

Israel—A Spiritual Travel Guide, 2nd Edition: A Companion for the Modern Jewish Pilgrim
By Rabbi Lawrence A. Hoffman 4¼ x 10, 256 pp, Quality PB, illus., ISBN 1-58023-261-2 **$18.99**
Also Available: **The Israel Mission Leader's Guide** ISBN 1-58023-085-7 **$4.95**

12 Steps

100 Blessings Every Day Daily Twelve Step Recovery Affirmations, Exercises for Personal Growth & Renewal Reflecting Seasons of the Jewish Year
By Rabbi Kerry M. Olitzky. Foreword by Rabbi Neil Gillman.
One-day-at-a-time monthly format. Reflects on the rhythm of the Jewish calendar to bring insight to recovery from addictions.
4½ x 6½, 432 pp, Quality PB, ISBN 1-879045-30-3 **$15.99**

Recovery from Codependence: A Jewish Twelve Steps Guide to Healing Your Soul
By Rabbi Kerry M. Olitzky 6 x 9, 160 pp, Quality PB, ISBN 1-879045-32-X **$13.95**

Renewed Each Day: Daily Twelve Step Recovery Meditations Based on the Bible
By Rabbi Kerry M. Olitzky and Aaron Z.
Vol. 1—Genesis & Exodus: 6 x 9, 224 pp, Quality PB, ISBN 1-879045-12-5 **$14.95**
Vol. 2—Leviticus, Numbers & Deuteronomy: 6 x 9, 280 pp, Quality PB, ISBN 1-879045-13-3 **$18.99**

Twelve Jewish Steps to Recovery: A Personal Guide to Turning from Alcoholism & Other Addictions—Drugs, Food, Gambling, Sex...
By Rabbi Kerry M. Olitzky and Stuart A. Copans, M.D. Preface by Abraham J. Twerski, M.D.
6 x 9, 144 pp, Quality PB, ISBN 1-879045-09-5 **$14.95**

Meditation

The Handbook of Jewish Meditation Practices
A Guide for Enriching the Sabbath and Other Days of Your Life
By Rabbi David A. Cooper
Easy-to-learn meditation techniques. 6 x 9, 208 pp, Quality PB, ISBN 1-58023-102-0 **$16.95**

Discovering Jewish Meditation: Instruction & Guidance for Learning an Ancient
Spiritual Practice *By Nan Fink Gefen, Ph.D.* 6 x 9, 208 pp, Quality PB, ISBN 1-58023-067-9 **$16.95**

A Heart of Stillness: A Complete Guide to Learning the Art of Meditation
By Rabbi David A. Cooper 5½ x 8½, 272 pp, Quality PB, ISBN 1-893361-03-9 **$16.95**
(A SkyLight Paths book)

Meditation from the Heart of Judaism: Today's Teachers Share Their
Practices, Techniques, and Faith *Edited by Avram Davis*
6 x 9, 256 pp, Quality PB, ISBN 1-58023-049-0 **$16.95**

Silence, Simplicity & Solitude: A Complete Guide to Spiritual Retreat at Home
By Rabbi David A. Cooper 5½ x 8½, 336 pp, Quality PB, ISBN 1-893361-04-7 **$16.95**
(A SkyLight Paths book)

The Way of Flame: A Guide to the Forgotten Mystical Tradition of Jewish
Meditation *By Avram Davis* 4½ x 8, 176 pp, Quality PB, ISBN 1-58023-060-1 **$15.95**

Ritual/Sacred Practice/Journaling

The Jewish Dream Book: The Key to Opening the Inner Meaning of
Your Dreams *By Vanessa L. Ochs with Elizabeth Ochs; Full-color illus. by Kristina Swarner*
Instructions for how modern people can perform ancient Jewish dream practices
and dream interpretations drawn from the Jewish wisdom tradition. For anyone
who wants to understand their dreams—and themselves.
8 x 8, 120 pp, Full-color illus., Deluxe PB w/flaps, ISBN 1-58023-132-2 **$16.95**

The Jewish Journaling Book: How to Use Jewish Tradition to Write
Your Life & Explore Your Soul *By Janet Ruth Falon*
Details the history of Jewish journaling throughout biblical and modern times,
and teaches specific journaling techniques to help you create and maintain a vital
journal, from a Jewish perspective. 8 x 8, 304 pp, Deluxe PB w/flaps, ISBN 1-58023-203-5 **$18.99**

The Book of Jewish Sacred Practices: CLAL's Guide to Everyday & Holiday
Rituals & Blessings *Edited by Rabbi Irwin Kula and Vanessa L. Ochs, Ph.D.*
6 x 9, 368 pp, Quality PB, ISBN 1-58023-152-7 **$18.95**

Jewish Ritual: A Brief Introduction for Christians
By Rabbi Kerry M. Olitzky and Rabbi Daniel Judson
5½ x 8½, 144 pp, Quality PB, ISBN 1-58023-210-8 **$14.99**

The Rituals & Practices of a Jewish Life: A Handbook for Personal Spiritual
Renewal *Edited by Rabbi Kerry M. Olitzky and Rabbi Daniel Judson*
6 x 9, 272 pp, illus., Quality PB, ISBN 1-58023-169-1 **$18.95**

Science Fiction/
Mystery & Detective Fiction

Mystery Midrash: An Anthology of Jewish Mystery & Detective Fiction
Edited by Lawrence W. Raphael. Preface by Joel Siegel.
6 x 9, 304 pp, Quality PB, ISBN 1-58023-055-5 **$16.95**

Criminal Kabbalah: An Intriguing Anthology of Jewish Mystery & Detective Fiction
Edited by Lawrence W. Raphael. Foreword by Laurie R. King.
6 x 9, 256 pp, Quality PB, ISBN 1-58023-109-8 **$16.95**

Wandering Stars: An Anthology of Jewish Fantasy & Science Fiction
Edited by Jack Dann. Introduction by Isaac Asimov.
6 x 9, 272 pp, Quality PB, ISBN 1-58023-005-9 **$16.95**

More Wandering Stars: An Anthology of Outstanding Stories of Jewish Fantasy and
Science Fiction *Edited by Jack Dann. Introduction by Isaac Asimov.*
6 x 9, 192 pp, Quality PB, ISBN 1-58023-063-6 **$16.95**

Spirituality

Does the Soul Survive? A Jewish Journey to Belief in Afterlife, Past Lives & Living with Purpose *By Rabbi Elie Kaplan Spitz. Foreword by Brian L Weiss, M.D.*
Spitz relates his own experiences and those shared with him by people he has worked with as a rabbi, and shows us that belief in afterlife and past lives, so often approached with reluctance, is in fact true to Jewish tradition.
6 x 9, 288 pp, Quality PB, ISBN 1-58023-165-9 **$16.95**; Hardcover, ISBN 1-58023-094-6 **$21.95**

First Steps to a New Jewish Spirit: Reb Zalman's Guide to Recapturing the Intimacy & Ecstasy in Your Relationship with God
By Rabbi Zalman M. Schachter-Shalomi with Donald Gropman
An extraordinary spiritual handbook that restores psychic and physical vigor by introducing us to new models and alternative ways of practicing Judaism. Offers meditation and contemplation exercises for enriching the most important aspects of everyday life. 6 x 9, 144 pp, Quality PB, ISBN 1-58023-182-9 **$16.95**

God in Our Relationships: Spirituality between People from the Teachings of Martin Buber *By Rabbi Dennis S. Ross*
On the eightieth anniversary of Buber's classic work, we can discover new answers to critical issues in our lives. Inspiring examples from Ross's own life—as congregational rabbi, father, hospital chaplain, social worker, and husband—illustrate Buber's difficult-to-understand ideas about how we encounter God and each other. 5½ x 8½, 160 pp, Quality PB, ISBN 1-58023-147-0 **$16.95**

Judaism, Physics and God: Searching for Sacred Metaphors in a Post-Einstein World *By Rabbi David W. Nelson*
In clear, non-technical terms, this provocative study examines the great theories of modern physics to find new ways for contemporary people to express their spiritual beliefs and thoughts.
6 x 9, 352 pp, Hardcover, ISBN 1-58023-252-3 **$24.99**

The Jewish Lights Spirituality Handbook: A Guide to Understanding, Exploring & Living a Spiritual Life *Edited by Stuart M. Matlins*
What exactly is "Jewish" about spirituality? How do I make it a part of my life? Fifty of today's foremost spiritual leaders share their ideas and experience with us.
6 x 9, 456 pp, Quality PB, ISBN 1-58023-093-8 **$19.95**; Hardcover, ISBN 1-58023-100-4 **$24.95**

Bringing the Psalms to Life: How to Understand and Use the Book of Psalms
By Dr. Daniel F. Polish
6 x 9, 208 pp, Quality PB, ISBN 1-58023-157-8 **$16.95**; Hardcover, ISBN 1-58023-077-6 **$21.95**

God & the Big Bang: Discovering Harmony between Science & Spirituality
By Dr. Daniel C. Matt 6 x 9, 216 pp, Quality PB, ISBN 1-879045-89-3 **$16.95**

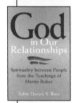

Godwrestling—Round 2: Ancient Wisdom, Future Paths
By Rabbi Arthur Waskow 6 x 9, 352 pp, Quality PB, ISBN 1-879045-72-9 **$18.95**

One God Clapping: The Spiritual Path of a Zen Rabbi *By Rabbi Alan Lew with Sherril Jaffe*
5¼ x 8¼, 336 pp, Quality PB, ISBN 1-58023-115-2 **$16.95**

Six Jewish Spiritual Paths: A Rationalist Looks at Spirituality *By Rabbi Rifat Sonsino*
6 x 9, 208 pp, Quality PB, ISBN 1-58023-167-5 **$16.95**; Hardcover, ISBN 1-58023-095-4 **$21.95**

Soul Judaism: Dancing with God into a New Era
By Rabbi Wayne Dosick 5½ x 8½, 304 pp, Quality PB, ISBN 1-58023-053-9 **$16.95**

Stepping Stones to Jewish Spiritual Living: Walking the Path Morning, Noon, and Night *By Rabbi James L. Mirel and Karen Bonnell Werth*
6 x 9, 240 pp, Quality PB, ISBN 1-58023-074-1 **$16.95**; Hardcover, ISBN 1-58023-003-2 **$21.95**

There Is No Messiah … and You're It: The Stunning Transformation of Judaism's Most Provocative Idea *By Rabbi Robert N. Levine, D.D.*
6 x 9, 192 pp, Quality PB, ISBN 1-58023-255-8 **$16.99**; Hardcover, ISBN 1-58023-173-X **$21.95**

These Are the Words: A Vocabulary of Jewish Spiritual Life *By Dr. Arthur Green*
6 x 9, 304 pp, Quality PB, ISBN 1-58023-107-1 **$18.95**

Spirituality/The Way Into... Series

The Way Into... Series offers an accessible and highly usable "guided tour" of the Jewish faith, people, history and beliefs—in total, an introduction to Judaism that will enable you to understand and interact with the sacred texts of the Jewish tradition. Each volume is written by a leading contemporary scholar and teacher, and explores one key aspect of Judaism. *The Way Into...* enables all readers to achieve a real sense of Jewish cultural literacy through guided study.

The Way Into Encountering God in Judaism *By Neil Gillman*
6 x 9, 240 pp, Quality PB, ISBN 1-58023-199-3 **$18.99**; Hardcover, ISBN 1-58023-025-3 **$21.95**
Also Available: **The Jewish Approach to God: A Brief Introduction for Christians**
By Neil Gillman 5½ x 8½, 192 pp, Quality PB, ISBN 1-58023-190-X **$16.95**

The Way Into Jewish Mystical Tradition *By Lawrence Kushner*
6 x 9, 224 pp, Quality PB, ISBN 1-58023-200-0 **$18.99**; Hardcover, ISBN 1-58023-029-6 **$21.95**

The Way Into Jewish Prayer *By Lawrence A. Hoffman*
6 x 9, 224 pp, Quality PB, ISBN 1-58023-201-9 **$18.99**; Hardcover, ISBN 1-58023-027-X **$21.95**

The Way Into the Relationship between Jews and Non-Jews: Searching for
Boundaries and Bridges *By Michael A. Signer, PhD*
6 x 9, 225 pp (est.), Hardcover, ISBN 1-58023-267-1 **$24.99**

The Way Into Judaism and the Environment *By Jeremy Benstein, PhD*
6 x 9, 225 pp (est.), Hardcover, ISBN 1-58023-268-X **$24.99**

The Way Into Tikkun Olam (Repairing the World) *By Elliot N. Dorff*
6 x 9, 320 pp, Hardcover, ISBN 1-58023-269-8 **$24.99**

The Way Into Torah *By Norman J. Cohen*
6 x 9, 176 pp, Quality PB, ISBN 1-58023-198-5 **$16.99**; Hardcover, ISBN 1-58023-028-8 **$21.95**

Spirituality and Wellness

Aleph-Bet Yoga
Embodying the Hebrew Letters for Physical and Spiritual Well-Being
By Steven A. Rapp. Foreword by Tamar Frankiel, Ph.D., and Judy Greenfeld. Preface by Hart Lazer
7 x 10, 128 pp, b/w photos, Quality PB, Layflat binding, ISBN 1-58023-162-4 **$16.95**

Entering the Temple of Dreams
Jewish Prayers, Movements, and Meditations for the End of the Day
By Tamar Frankiel, Ph.D., and Judy Greenfeld
7 x 10, 192 pp, illus., Quality PB, ISBN 1-58023-079-2 **$16.95**

Jewish Paths toward Healing and Wholeness: A Personal Guide to Dealing
with Suffering *By Rabbi Kerry M. Olitzky. Foreword by Debbie Friedman.*
6 x 9, 192 pp, Quality PB, ISBN 1-58023-068-7 **$15.95**

Minding the Temple of the Soul
Balancing Body, Mind, and Spirit through Traditional Jewish Prayer, Movement, and
Meditation *By Tamar Frankiel, Ph.D., and Judy Greenfeld*
7 x 10, 184 pp, illus., Quality PB, ISBN 1-879045-64-8 **$16.95**
Audiotape of the Blessings and Meditations: 60 min. **$9.95**
Videotape of the Movements and Meditations: 46 min. **$20.00**

Spirituality/Lawrence Kushner

Filling Words with Light: Hasidic and Mystical Reflections on Jewish Prayer
By Lawrence Kushner and Nehemia Polen
Reflects on the joy, gratitude, mystery and awe embedded in traditional prayers and blessings, and shows how you can imbue these familiar sacred words with your own sense of holiness. 5¼ x 8½, 176 pp, Hardcover, ISBN 1-58023-216-7 **$21.99**

The Book of Letters: A Mystical Hebrew Alphabet
Popular Hardcover Edition, 6 x 9, 80 pp, 2-color text, ISBN 1-879045-00-1 **$24.95**
Collector's Limited Edition, 9 x 12, 80 pp, gold foil embossed pages, w/limited edition silkscreened print, ISBN 1-879045-04-4 **$349.00**

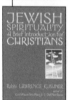

The Book of Miracles: A Young Person's Guide to Jewish Spiritual Awareness
6 x 9, 96 pp, 2-color illus., Hardcover, ISBN 1-879045-78-8 **$16.95** *For ages 9–13*

The Book of Words: Talking Spiritual Life, Living Spiritual Talk
6 x 9, 160 pp, Quality PB, ISBN 1-58023-020-2 **$16.95**

Eyes Remade for Wonder: A Lawrence Kushner Reader *Introduction by Thomas Moore*
6 x 9, 240 pp, Quality PB, ISBN 1-58023-042-3 **$18.95**; Hardcover, ISBN 1-58023-014-8 **$23.95**

God Was in This Place & I, i Did Not Know
Finding Self, Spirituality and Ultimate Meaning 6 x 9, 192 pp, Quality PB, ISBN 1-879045-33-8 **$16.95**

Honey from the Rock: An Introduction to Jewish Mysticism
6 x 9, 176 pp, Quality PB, ISBN 1-58023-073-3 **$16.95**

Invisible Lines of Connection: Sacred Stories of the Ordinary
5¼ x 8½, 160 pp, Quality PB, ISBN 1-879045-98-2 **$15.95**

Jewish Spirituality—A Brief Introduction for Christians
5¼ x 8½, 112 pp, Quality PB Original, ISBN 1-58023-150-0 **$12.95**

The River of Light: Jewish Mystical Awareness 6 x 9, 192 pp, Quality PB, ISBN 1-58023-096-2 **$16.95**

The Way Into Jewish Mystical Tradition
6 x 9, 224 pp, Quality PB, ISBN 1-58023-200-0 **$18.99**; Hardcover, ISBN 1-58023-029-6 **$21.95**

Spirituality/Prayer

Pray Tell: A Hadassah Guide to Jewish Prayer
By Rabbi Jules Harlow, with contributions from Tamara Cohen, Rochelle Furstenberg, Rabbi Daniel Gordis, Leora Tanenbaum, and many others
Enriched with insight and wisdom from a broad variety of viewpoints.
8½ x 11, 400 pp, Quality PB, ISBN 1-58023-163-2 **$29.95**

My People's Prayer Book Series

Traditional Prayers, Modern Commentaries   *Edited by Rabbi Lawrence A. Hoffman*
Provides diverse and exciting commentary to the traditional liturgy, helping modern men and women find new wisdom in Jewish prayer, and bring liturgy into their lives. Each book includes Hebrew text, modern translation, and commentaries from all perspectives of the Jewish world.

Vol. 1—The *Sh'ma* and Its Blessings
7 x 10, 168 pp, Hardcover, ISBN 1-879045-79-6 **$24.99**
Vol. 2—The *Amidah*
7 x 10, 240 pp, Hardcover, ISBN 1-879045-80-X **$24.95**
Vol. 3—*P'sukei D'zimrah* (Morning Psalms)
7 x 10, 240 pp, Hardcover, ISBN 1-879045-81-8 **$24.95**
Vol. 4—*Seder K'riat Hatorah* (The Torah Service)
7 x 10, 264 pp, Hardcover, ISBN 1-879045-82-6 **$23.95**
Vol. 5—*Birkhot Hashachar* (Morning Blessings)
7 x 10, 240 pp, Hardcover, ISBN 1-879045-83-4 **$24.95**
Vol. 6—*Tachanun* and Concluding Prayers
7 x 10, 240 pp, Hardcover, ISBN 1-879045-84-2 **$24.95**
Vol. 7—Shabbat at Home
7 x 10, 240 pp, Hardcover, ISBN 1-879045-85-0 **$24.95**
Vol. 8—*Kabbalat Shabbat* (Welcoming Shabbat in the Synagogue)
7 x 10, 240 pp, Hardcover, ISBN 1-58023-121-7 **$24.99**
Vol. 9—Welcoming the Night: *Minchah* and *Ma'ariv* (Afternoon and Evening Prayer) 7 x 10, 272 pp, Hardcover, ISBN 1-58023-262-0 **$24.99**

Theology/Philosophy

About Jewish Lights

People of all faiths and backgrounds yearn for books that attract, engage, educate, and spiritually inspire.

Our principal goal is to stimulate thought and help all people learn about who the Jewish People are, where they come from, and what the future can be made to hold. While people of our diverse Jewish heritage are the primary audience, our books speak to people in the Christian world as well and will broaden their understanding of Judaism and the roots of their own faith.

We bring to you authors who are at the forefront of spiritual thought and experience. While each has something different to say, they all say it in a voice that you can hear.

Our books are designed to welcome you and then to engage, stimulate, and inspire. We judge our success not only by whether or not our books are beautiful and commercially successful, but by whether or not they make a difference in your life.

For your information and convenience, at the back of this book we have provided a list of other Jewish Lights books you might find interesting and useful. They cover all the categories of your life:

Stuart M. Matlins, Publisher